Jesus *and* Jihad

Jesus *and* Jihad

Reclaiming the Prophetic Heart of Christianity and Islam

ROBERT F. SHEDINGER

 CASCADE *Books* · Eugene, Oregon

JESUS AND JIHAD
Reclaiming the Prophetic Heart of Christianity and Islam

Cascade Books
An Imprint of Wipf and Stock Publishers
199 W. 8th Ave., Suite 3
Eugene, OR 97401

www.wipfandstock.com

ISBN 13: 978-1-4982-2021-7

Cataloguing-in-Publication Data

Shedinger, Robert F.

    Jesus and jihad : reclaiming the prophetic heart of Christianity and Islam / Robert F. Shedinger.

    x + 166 p. ; 23 cm. Includes bibliographical references.

    ISBN 13: 978-1-4982-2021-7

    1. Religion—Philosophy. 2. Social Justice—Religious aspects—Christianity. 3. Social Justice—Religious aspects—Islam. I. Title.

HM271 .S33. 2015

Manufactured in the U.S.A.   05/20/2015

For all prophetic Muslims currently denied the right to due process

Contents

Acknowledgments

I never thought I would write a book titled *Jesus and Jihad*. That I have is a testament to all those Christians and Muslims who have inspired me with their uncompromising dedication to social action in the pursuit of justice. Special thanks are due to Mustapha Elturk and the members of the Islamic Organization of North America for all their friendship and support, and for their making me aware of the extraordinary work of Dr. Israr Ahmad.

Thanks are due also to Zulfiqar Ali Shah and Ahmed Afzaal for their inspirational concern for justice and peace, and to Sayyid Qazi for showing me that Las Vegas is much more than just the playground for the rich and powerful.

If it were not for the wonderful work of John Kiser, Kathy Garms, and all those associated with the Abd el-Kader Education Project, I would know nothing about this great nineteenth-century Algerian who embodies the spirit of jihad at its very best and whose name so improbably adorns a small Iowa town.

I must also thank Mel Underbakke of the National Coalition to Protect Civil Freedoms, both for reading the manuscript, and for making me aware of the plight of Muslims being preemptively prosecuted and imprisoned without access to due process. The tireless advocacy of Mel and her husband, Fred, in support of these innocent victims of America's War on Terror is truly inspiring.

I cannot say enough about the intellectually stimulating atmosphere of Luther College and the collegewide concern for activism leading to justice and peace. I have learned so much from so many students over the years. I owe them a huge debt of gratitude, along with the many faculty colleagues who have been an inspiration. Thanks especially to Todd Green,

Acknowledgments

who is always a particularly insightful conversation partner on the plight of Muslims in the contemporary West.

Thanks also must go to the many wonderful examples of prophetic Christianity who worship in my home church, First United Methodist Church in Decorah, Iowa—especially to Rev. Jim and Barb Dale, whose lives embody what it means to follow a Jesus who demands justice; and thanks also to Rev. Dr. John Caldwell, whose preaching brings a prophetic Jesus alive in the pulpit Sunday after Sunday.

I also must thank all of the dedicated professionals at Cascade Books, who make the experience of publishing so easy and stress free. I especially thank K. C. Hanson for believing in the value of this book.

Finally, I thank my family: Tina, whose loving support means everything; Tyler, whose growing interest in golf gives me a welcome respite from books and academia; and Amey, my book writing companion, who will undoubtedly publish her own work someday.

1

Introduction

We cannot solve our problems with
the same level of thinking that created them.

—Albert Einstein

Few words possess more power to inspire fear and loathing in the average American these days than *jihad*. Its mere utterance conjures up images of car bombs exploding in crowded markets, of Boeing 737s crashing into tall buildings, and of flag-burning, gun-toting bearded Arab men shouting *"Allahu akbar!"* and "Death to America!" *Jihad* is almost universally thought to mean "holy war," a military venture waged by primitive Muslim extremists bent on conquering freedom-loving Americans in order to enslave them under an Islamic theocracy based on shariah law. Given the prevalence of this overwhelmingly negative caricature of jihad, a creative new interpretation recently offered by an American-born Muslim man in a Boston courtroom is almost sure to offend American patriotic sensibilities to their very core. Who are we talking about?

His name is Tarek Mehanna, and in April of 2012 during a hearing in which he was sentenced to a seventeen-year federal prison term for allegedly expressing sympathy with Islamic extremists, he had the audacity to characterize the American Revolution as a jihad! Such a seemingly outrageous characterization will likely have the same effect on American ears as the scratching of fingernails on a chalkboard. Yet despite its near-heretical nature, I believe Mehanna's understanding of jihad has the power to point us in the direction of a more just, peaceful, and sustainable future. I realize just how counterintuitive this sounds—jihad as a path to peace?—so please let me explain.

For those unfamiliar with this case, Tarek Mehanna is an American-born Muslim pharmacist sentenced to seventeen years in federal prison for allegedly expressing sympathy for al-Qaeda and conspiring to kill U.S. soldiers in Iraq. No evidence exists linking Mehanna to any actual terrorist activities. He was simply charged with translating certain Arabic documents found on the Internet into English and expressing sympathy with what the U.S. government brands terrorist organizations. Because of Mehanna's status as a natural-born American citizen, some protested his sentencing, alleging it to be politically motivated and a violation of Mehanna's constitutional right to free speech. That Tarek Mehanna was preemptively prosecuted and sentenced to prison is, however, hardly noteworthy even if it is constitutionally troublesome: this happens to Muslims all too routinely these days. But my purpose here is not to focus on Mehanna's guilt or innocence, but rather to focus on the extraordinary statement he delivered to the court at his sentencing hearing.[1]

Mehanna begins by asserting that the FBI had tried to hire him as an informant against possible terrorist organizations. If the FBI had hired him as an informant, Mehanna would have been granted immunity from prosecution. But when he declined to provide the requested information to the FBI, Mehanna claims, he was arrested and charged with the crime of, in his words, "supporting the mujahideen fighting the occupation of Muslim countries around the world. Or as they like to call them, 'terrorists.'" As someone born and bred in America (and in the patriotic milieu of Boston, no less), how could Mehanna come to support Islamic extremists who exacted such a heavy toll on his fellow American citizens? Are the charges against him legitimate? This is where Mehanna's statement takes a most unexpected turn.

When he is questioned about how he could believe the things he believes or take the positions he takes, Mehanna's shocking reply is that it is *because* of his American upbringing that he is who he is! To clarify this astonishing assertion, Mehanna launches into a long discourse about what he

---

1. The text of Mehanna's statement appears online in Greenwald, "Real Criminals."

learned through his years in the American public school system, and about how that educational experience transformed him into a sympathizer with so-called Islamic terrorists. Viewing his American education as a source for his support of Islamic extremists might seem outrageous at first. But let's hear Mehanna out before passing hasty judgment. Mehanna's argument is really quite compelling.

Mehanna begins by taking us back to when he was six years old and collecting Batman comic books like any other six-year-old American child. He learned early on from these comic books that the world is set up in a particular way: "there are oppressors, there are the oppressed, and there are those who step up to defend the oppressed." This idea resonated so much that as he grew, he gravitated towards books that reflected this theme—books like *Uncle Tom's Cabin*, *The Autobiography of Malcolm X*, and other classics of American literature (even *The Catcher in the Rye*). By the time he was studying history in high school, Mehanna realized just how real this theme was as he learned about what befell the American Indians at the hands of European settlers, and in turn how the European settlers were oppressed by King George III. He read about Paul Revere, Thomas Paine, and the armed insurgency of American colonialists against the tyranny of the British crown. He learned about Harriet Tubman, Nat Turner, and John Brown in the struggle against slavery. He learned about Emma Goldman, Eugene Debs, and the development of the labor movement. He learned about Rosa Parks, Malcolm X, Martin Luther King Jr., and the civil rights struggle. But Mehanna did not see this theme of the struggle against oppression reflected only in American history.

He learned also about Anne Frank and the Nazis, Ho Chi Minh and the fight for Vietnamese independence, and Nelson Mandela and the struggle against apartheid in South Africa. In every one of these examples of the struggle for justice, Mehanna found himself regularly siding with the oppressed and respecting those who intervened on the side of the marginalized of society regardless of their nationality or religion. The one figure that really stood out to him was Malcolm X. Mehanna was impressed with the fundamental transformation that Malcolm underwent in his life—from hardened criminal to leader of his people and a disciplined Muslim performing the *hajj* to Mecca. Malcolm's life taught Mehanna that "Islam is not something inherited; it's not a culture or ethnicity. It's a way of life, a state of mind anyone can choose no matter where they come from or how they were raised." Through his study of Malcolm X, Mehanna began to delve deeper into Islam, and there he found the answer to the question that stumped the greatest scientific minds: the question that drives the rich and famous to depression and suicide from being unable to answer: What is the purpose of life? Why do we exist in this universe?

Soon Mehanna found himself valuing Islam "like a piece of gold" and turning his attention to the trials befalling Muslims in other parts of the world. He learned what the Soviets had done to the Muslims of Afghanistan, what the Serbs had done to the Muslims of Bosnia, what the Russians were doing to the Muslims of Chechnya, and what Israel had done in Lebanon and Palestine with the full backing of the U.S. government. Further, he learned about what America had itself done to Muslims: about the sanctions against Iraq that killed more than a half million children; and he learned that then-Secretary of State Madeleine Albright famously passed off the deaths of these children as "worth it" in a noteworthy *60 Minutes* interview. Mehanna learned about the slaughter of twenty-four Muslim civilians in Haditha by U.S. Marines; about Abeer al-Janabi, a fourteen-year-old Iraqi girl gang-raped by five American soldiers who then shot her and her family and set their corpses on fire; about the drone strikes that killed innocent Muslim civilians in Pakistan, Somalia, and Yemen. Mehanna's sympathy with the oppressed became more acute and more personal as he witnessed the fate of his fellow Muslims at the hands of his own government.

But reflecting back on his own American roots once again, Mehanna follows with likely his most shocking statement of all:

> I mentioned Paul Revere—when he went on his midnight ride, it was for the purpose of warning the people that the British were marching to Lexington to arrest Sam Adams and John Hancock, then on to Concord to confiscate the weapons stored there by the Minuteman [*sic*]. By the time they got to Concord, they found the Minuteman [*sic*] waiting for them, weapons in hand. They fired at the British, fought them, and beat them. From that battle came the American Revolution. There's an Arabic word to describe what those Minutemen did that day. That word is: JIHAD, and this is what my trial was about.

Can this seeming frontal assault on American patriotic identity really be taken seriously? Or is Mehanna just trying to provoke American ire?

Many will conclude the latter, but I would opt for the former; for I believe that Mehanna's equating of one of the most detested ideas in contemporary public discourse with a foundational event of American patriotic nostalgia actually makes good sense. The American Revolution does accord quite well with the meaning of *jihad* as jihad is represented in the Qur'an and the works of many important Muslim scholars. In fact, I will go Mehanna one better and argue that, not only is jihad a good characterization of the American Revolution, but it is also a perfect lens through which to focus the life and work of Jesus of Nazareth—hence, the title of this book: *Jesus and Jihad.*

At this point, some readers will be ready to consign this book to the flames. But before warming your hands by the fire, consider the following: Jihad is simply not what the hysterical fearmongers want us to believe it is. By linking Jesus with jihad, I assure you I am not arguing that Jesus was a terrorist with no regard for the sanctity of human life! Quite the contrary. My purpose here is to reframe jihad, to rescue it from its hysterical Fox News–driven misrepresentations, and to recover it as a concept with the power to restore a prophetic heart to both Christianity and Islam—a prophetic heart in tremendous danger of being lost from both traditions much to the detriment of a world suffering under unspeakably inhumane systems of injustice. Viewed for its prophetic character, the Jesus/jihad connection should not appear so threatening. Still, some readers will be asking how such a universally vilified concept as jihad could ever be considered a force for justice—and a description of the mission of Jesus no less! But before I engage this question, please note that I am not alone in my belief in the profoundly helpful nature of Tarek Mehanna's interpretation of jihad.

A few days after Mehanna's sentencing hearing, Ross Caputi published a blog post titled "If Tarek Mehanna is Guilty So Am I."[2] What makes Caputi's support for Mehanna so noteworthy is that Caputi is a former U.S. combat marine who served in Iraq between 2003 and 2006. He fought in the battle for Fallujah in November 2004 and witnessed the deaths of several of his close friends at the hands of the Iraqi mujahideen. How could Caputi possibly find sympathy with Mehanna's support for those who killed his fellow marines? On Caputi's reading, all Mehanna is really guilty of is believing that Muslims have a right to defend themselves against outside invaders, just as any other people do. If this is a crime, Caputi confesses to sharing that guilt: "I too support the right of Muslims to defend themselves against U.S. troops, even if that means they have to kill them." Caputi even accepts Mehanna's wider understanding of the meaning of *jihad* and asserts, "most Americans would be shocked to learn that they share many

2. Caputi's blog post appears online at www.commondreams.org/view/2012/04/16–13?

values with Jihadists, like duty, the importance of self-improvement, and the right to self-defense."

Indeed, Americans in general—even American Christians—*will* be shocked at how much they hold in common with an idea as vilified as jihad. If a combat marine who witnessed the deaths of close friends at the hands of jihad-waging Muslims can nevertheless find common cause with Mehanna's support of those same jihadists, maybe the rest of us ought to approach this issue with a considerably more open mind. There is much that we do not understand about jihad. I seek to correct the record.

Allow me then to sketch out in broad outline the steps in my argument equating Jesus with jihad in order to demonstrate the idea's potential merits. Subsequent chapters will then fill in the details to hopefully render the argument convincing. But whether my argument is convincing or not, we do have to realize that the common American perception of jihad as a holy war designed to spread Islamic influence to the far corners of the earth while destroying a Christian America has little basis in Islamic teachings and is nothing more than a harmful stereotype conjured up by well-funded Islamophobic networks in the West who seize on the ideas perpetuated by a minuscule minority of Muslim preachers in order to impugn the reputation of a diverse and complex tradition in its entirety. Nathan Lean brilliantly analyzes the highly coordinated character of this movement in his aptly titled book *The Islamophobia Industry: How the Right Manufactures Fear of Muslims*. Michele Bachmann, Pamela Geller, Robert Spencer, Daniel Pipes, and other high-profile Islamophobic figures may get the media attention they crave with their hysterical rantings about an imminent Muslim threat, but their knowledge of Islam appears to run about as deep as a rain puddle evaporating in the July sun. My purpose is to provide a much deeper and more nuanced discussion of Islam and jihad than is available from these fearmongering media darlings.

If we can positively engage the concept of jihad as it emerges from Islamic sources and the works of Muslim thinkers, we may be able to find a key to dismantling the antipathy that currently colors the relationship between so many Americans and their Muslim neighbors. It won't be easy, but at least it is worth a try. Neither Christians nor Muslims will pass from the world stage anytime soon. Learning to live and work together is the only possible path to a peaceful future.

Introduction

CONNECTING JESUS AND JIHAD

What does it mean to make the provocative—but nevertheless serious—claim that Jesus waged a jihad? And what does it mean to argue that embracing this Jesus/jihad connection may hold the key to reclaiming the prophetic heart of both Christianity and Islam—a prophetic heart in serious decline in both traditions, much to the detriment of a world in desperate need of a prophetic movement toward the establishment of justice and peace? Let me begin with the second question by considering the evidence for the claim that the prophetic heart of Christianity and Islam is fast disappearing. This may not be a controversial idea, but it will help here to clarify precisely how I am using the term *prophetic*. Once we have done this, we can work back to a detailed discussion of the Jesus/jihad connection and its importance for any attempt to reclaim a prophetic heart in service to a hurting world.

What exactly is a prophetic heart? The concept of prophecy is related by many people to telling the future. A prophet is one who makes predictions about the unfolding of future events, especially events of historic magnitude. Many times the term *prophecy* is used to describe speculations about the end of the world. Prophets are those who make end-time predictions or who try to discern the signs of the last days, like Hal Lindsey in his book *The Late Great Planet Earth*. This idea of the prophet as apocalyptic fortuneteller is a modern invention, however. When I speak of the prophetic, I am thinking of the way prophets functioned in the Bible—not as fortunetellers but as those who spoke truth to power. Biblical prophets primarily acted as social critics, prophetic disturbers who called their people to account for their ethical lapses and predicted the divine wrath that would result. It is in this sense of making prophetic disturbance that I think the prophetic heart of Christianity and Islam is quickly slipping away.

What is the evidence for this? Well, consider the following. The parts of the world where either Christianity or Islam is the dominant religion (and this is a significant part of the world) are struggling under the weight of all kinds of social and economic injustices. Though Christianity may boast more than two billion adherents worldwide, and Islam 1.5 billion, the societies where these two largest religious traditions dominate are rife with ethical lapses of the most heinous kinds, such as growing wealth inequalities that allow the rich to exploit the poor (think the United States); authoritarian political structures that brutally oppress their own citizens (think Syria); gender inequalities and misogynistic structures that spell

7

misery for women (think many countries); racial and ethnic animus that fragments the human family and leads to violence and warfare (think too many countries); and the raping and pillaging of the natural world, which threatens to destroy the very environment that renders human life possible (think everywhere). With so many Christians and Muslims living in these societies and under these conditions, where are the voices of the prophetic disturbers calling the powerful to account for these ethical failures? Where is the struggle to transform these societies into more just and peaceful ones along the lines that Christians and Muslims both profess has been ordained by God? Christians even repeatedly pray for God's kingdom to become a reality on earth (as it is in heaven), but where are the Christians actively engaged in trying to bring about this prayed-for transformation? Such prophetic voices do exist, of course (Pope Francis, for example), but they are becoming increasingly difficult to hear as they dwindle to the status of being the noteworthy exception rather than the rule.

Sadly, the vast majority of the world's Christians and Muslims view Christianity and Islam respectively as individualized faith traditions whose primary purpose is personal spiritual enrichment, not social transformation designed to bring about justice and peace. Christianity, particularly in America, has been reduced to believing the "correct" church-approved doctrines, accepting Jesus as personal Lord and savior, and anticipating an eternity in heaven. Islam has been reduced to accepting the divinely revealed nature of the Qur'an and the Prophethood of Muhammad while performing the various rituals contained in the Five Pillars of the faith along with anticipating eternal bliss. For far too many Christians and Muslims today, being Christian or Muslim is about practicing a particular religion, and the mere suggestion that Christian and Muslim teachings have relevance for the larger political, economic, and social affairs of life brings howls of protest—especially the suggestion that the political, economic, and social aspects may actually be primary. "Religion is religion and politics is politics," we are told. "Politics and religion are distinct realms and must be kept separate," is the familiar refrain. After all, haven't you ever heard of the separation of church and state?

One of the primary reasons for this loss of the prophetic is the advancement of secularization around the world. Secularization is that process whereby societies create for themselves a conceptual dichotomy between supposedly sacred and secular realms. Once this conceptual dichotomy is in place, spiritual matters can be safely cordoned off in the sacred realm in

Introduction

a structure called religion, leaving behind a secular realm run according to the dictates of human reason, passion, and desire—the realm where political, economic, and social institutions operate. With spiritual matters safely cordoned off in the sacred realm, to resist having spiritual affairs be tainted by mundane affairs of everyday life becomes entirely logical. Religion is what we do in church on Sunday morning, not what we do at the office or at school on Monday; and we certainly would not want our spirituality to be compromised by the vagaries of political, economic, and social realities. Spirituality, we believe, has a purity quite distinct from the contingency of everyday life. Since this sacred/secular conceptual dichotomy so fundamental to Western thought now dominates our thinking, there is little motivation to exercise a prophetic voice. Making a prophetic critique of the secular powers that authorize injustice will get branded as abusing religion for political ends. (This charge is regularly leveled at Muslims who dare to reject the sacred/secular dichotomy.) The sacred and secular must not mix, we are told. They are completely heterogeneous realities, as Mircea Eliade so forcefully argued in his seminal book *The Sacred and the Profane*. But was Eliade right?

Scholars are coming to understand that far from being a neutral, universally valid description of reality, this sacred/secular binary worldview is actually the specific product of the Christian West, developing out of the European Enlightenment and the triumph of human reason. As globalization has fostered the spread of Western culture around the world, however, Muslim societies have become just as secularized as those in the West. With the diminishing volume of the prophetic voice, the human ego has been left largely unchecked to run roughshod over any concept of a just, equitable, and sustainable world. Christians and Muslims have been left, not only to accommodate to the unjust status quo as they go about their "religious" affairs, but in too many cases to reinterpret the central teachings of their traditions in such a way as to render them consistent with systems of injustice. How else to account for the alliance in America between evangelical Christians and the conservative political establishment whose policies enrich the wealthy while impoverishing the poor? Or the deeply entrenched Islamic identity of those fabulously wealthy (and unjust) petromonarchies in the Middle East? In far too many cases today, Christians and Muslims actively support political and economic policies that I firmly believe Jesus and Muhammad would have vehemently opposed. One of the few prophetic voices still active within Christianity, Cornel West, often raises the question of how we have become so adjusted to injustice. It is only when we grasp the profound truth at the heart of this question that we will be in a position to recover a prophetic heart that has largely gone AWOL.

The first step toward addressing the loss of this prophetic heart will be to reframe jihad and disentangle this central Islamic concept from the hysterical media-drive stereotypes that are used to inflame Islamophobic passions. Contrary to popular belief, *jihad* does not mean "holy war." Muslims are not plotting the overthrow of America. Muslims do not intend to try and force the whole world to become Muslim. This word that sparks so much fear and loathing in the average American is far more nuanced and interesting than most people realize.

Jihad comes from the Arabic root *jahada*, which means "to struggle or strive, to work hard at something." A jihad is simply a struggling or striving that is understood in an Islamic context as a striving in the way of God. What it means to strive in the way of God is unfortunately not spelled out with great clarity in the Qur'an, leading to the development of a variety of interpretations by Muslim thinkers over the centuries. For some, jihad means to strive within oneself to live a life in accordance with God's will. That is, jihad refers primarily to a personal spiritual struggle. For others, jihad refers to the struggle to defend oneself when attacked, and in this context often is understood as a kind of defensive warfare. For still others, jihad refers to the right to take the initiative to make real in history the just and equitable society at the heart of the Islamic vision. *Jihad* is a multivalent term, and it undoubtedly means all these things and more in the minds of many Muslims. There is no single definition of *jihad*. But there is also no essential equating of jihad with violence in Islamic sources either.

I don't want to be accused of sounding Pollyannaish here. The term *jihad* does include within its interpretive tradition the idea of violent warfare. The struggle to bring about just and equitable societies on earth may require the use of warfare, not unlike how America seeks to bring peace and democracy to Muslim countries through incredibly violent military action (shock-and-awe campaigns, to use military parlance). But jihad is not synonymous with war; the Qur'an always uses another term (*qatala*) when specifically referring to violent actions. *Jihad* has a much larger semantic range and has only been interpreted to mean "war" by some Islamic thinkers in particular circumstances.

What is perhaps most important to understand about jihad (and what is mostly ignored by Muslims themselves) is jihad's centrality to Muslim identity. The Qur'an makes it clear that to be a Muslim means to be engaged in jihad; jihad is not an optional activity. And I will later argue that in the Qur'an, the most natural understanding of jihad is to struggle and strive to bring about God's vision of a just and equitable society on earth. We must understand that the Qur'an arose in an environment where no meaningful separation between sacred and secular existed; secularization did not characterize seventh-century Arabia. The message of the Qur'an to live a life of full surrender to God was not just a personal spiritual or religious message; it was a call to bring all aspects of life under the purview of divine sovereignty—political, economic, and social institutions included. So the message of the Qur'an is necessarily political, and jihad should be understood as the necessity for Muslims to struggle and strive to bring about the political, economic, and social transformations envisioned in the Qur'an. Why is this envisioned as a struggle? *Because those who benefit from an unjust status quo will not surrender their power easily.* In short, to engage in jihad is to exercise one's prophetic voice. Without jihad, Islam devolves to a set of spiritual beliefs and practices fully accommodated to systems of injustice.

One person whose prophetic voice was heard loud and clear was Jesus of Nazareth. Despite a two-millennia-long tradition that has interpreted Jesus primarily as a spiritual savior (the proverbial Lamb of God who takes away the sins of the world), evidence continues to mount strongly indicating a highly prophetic (and therefore political) Jesus at work in first-century Roman Palestine. A full consideration of this evidence will come in a later chapter. Suffice it to say here that it was virtually impossible to be consigned to crucifixion in the first century without being considered a significant threat to the stability of the Roman political and economic order. The Romans used crucifixion specifically to intimidate subject populations into submission. There are much more efficient ways to execute someone than to let them linger on a cross for days on end! Besides, the very title attached to Jesus—Messiah—was essentially a military title referring to a coming kingly figure who would lead the final battle against Roman occupation of Judea and Galilee. I would go so far as to say that within the context of Roman political understanding, the crucifixion of Jesus was probably entirely justified. He likely *was* a threat to the empire.

As someone who proclaimed the coming of divine sovereignty on earth (the kingdom of God), Jesus could only have been understood to be rejecting Roman claims to be the true sovereign power over all the affairs of life. If the God of Israel is king, Caesar is not. There cannot be two sovereigns. Jesus's rejection of Roman claims to sovereignty clearly centered on the exploitative economic structures of the empire. The Jewish temple, which functioned as a Roman bank, became the focal point of Jesus's prophetic critique of imperial economics. This is the whole point of his anti-temple actions of overturning the tables of the moneychangers and driving out those who bought and sold in the temple court. Good evidence exists that Jesus rejected the paying of Roman tribute, and that he had garnered enough followers among the exploited poor to be seen as a threat to the Roman system. So they executed him. If Jesus's actions of prophetic struggle against exploitative imperial power in behalf of the poor and marginalized does not fit perfectly under the rubric of jihad, I don't know what does. Jesus, truly, was a mujahid—one who waged jihad.

Given the political nature of Jesus, what will it take for Christians and Muslims together to declare a responsible jihad against the structures of injustice threatening the last vestiges of human dignity and the sustainability of the entire planet? First, it will require that Christians and Muslims develop an understanding of their faith that does not contribute to the kinds of injustices they are called to resist. This is more difficult than it appears. For many Muslims and Christians, their faith traditions have devolved so far to the level of becoming only superficial identity markers, devoid of deep spiritual connection. So Christians and Muslims are increasingly becoming the victims of what we might call Religious-Identity Obsession Syndrome. This is an affliction characterized by a compulsive need to assert an exclusive claim to a particular religious identity seen as uniquely true and superior to all others. These superficial religious-identity claims then issue in exclusivist claims to absolute truth and in the rejection of and at times violent retribution towards those who hold differing views (think the Islamic State in Syria and Iraq [ISIS]). Religious intolerance is always born of fear, and fear is the outward expression of the existential anxiety that attends an inward loss of connection to deep spiritual resources (think ISIS again).

So no authentic jihad will be possible until Christians and Muslims can learn to transcend superficial religious-identity labels and connect to a deep well of spirituality wider than the narrow vision of any one particular confessional tradition. Whether it is at all possible for a significant number of Muslims and Christians to do this is highly debatable. Secularism has rendered it nearly impossible to truly believe in the existence of an immaterial reality. In the modern world, we have reinterpreted all phenomena as arising from the inanimate interplay of matter and energy. Our feelings and emotions are reduced to nothing more than the physical workings of our brain biochemistry. The spirit has been squeezed out of modern secular life. Yet, it is imperative that we try to transcend our narrowly conceived religious-identity labels and reengage the reality of our own psychic depths, for no authentically prophetic movement can arise apart from such a deep spiritual transformation. Fortunately, resources for how we might do this already exist within both the Islamic and Christian traditions. A first step will be to simply reengage those resources.

Christians and Muslims need to recognize the importance of spiritual development and (crucially) the connection between secularism and injustice. For example, ample evidence demonstrates that the great financial crisis of 2008 directly resulted from the secularization process. The world economy was nearly brought to its knees by those who had so lost all connection to a transcendent framework for life that the accumulation of material wealth at all costs seemed like the only reasonable way to live. Declaring a jihad against injustice will require an understanding of how secularism and the so-called separation of religion and politics serve to maintain systems of injustice. Muslims and Christians will need to embrace a prophetic stance rather than being cowed into submission by the pervasive rhetorical strategy that brands political action based on spiritual resources as an abuse of religion for political ends. Prophetic action is no such thing. Prophetic action is the pinnacle of spiritual development. It can be authentically engaged only by those who have matured beyond an adolescent obsession with superficial identity labels, beyond a notion of ideological purity, beyond a notion that material accumulation is the purpose of life, and beyond self-centered theological constructs that immunize us from the prophetic call to self-sacrifice in service to others.

Once an authentic prophetic heart is restored to Islam and Christianity, it will be time for Muslims and Christians together to wage a jihad against the many injustices of our time. Chief among these will be the struggle for economic justice. Secularization and globalization have effectively transferred power away from governments and have concentrated it in the hands of multinational corporations whose primary purpose is to maximize profits at the expense of human dignity. Instead of making money in return for manufacturing products or providing services of value, more and more, capitalists are bent on finding all kinds of creative ways to simply make money out of money—what Nobel Prize–winning economist Joseph Stiglitz calls "rent seeking." The rich get richer, but only by exploiting the poor. The Christian and Muslim traditions both have powerful resources to critique this system and envision a future of fairness and justice.

An authentic jihad will engage the ongoing struggle for racial and gender justice (Muslim feminist Amina Wadud even speaks of a "gender jihad"), environmental justice, and the search for a just peace. On this last point, peace can no longer be understood as simply the absence of war. True peace will only follow the establishment of justice. And the establishment of justice will be impossible without the active participation of Muslims, Christians, and others in the only kind of jihad worthy of this word's qur'anic definition.

This is the argument I will flesh out in detail in the chapters that follow. You may not buy it now—I don't really expect you to buy it now. But hopefully after you abide for a while in the more detailed discussions that lie ahead, you will come to see that jihad is not the scary idea that the Islamophobic fearmongers want us to believe it is. Rather, jihad may be the true path toward the more just and peaceful world we all want to live to see. In fact, embracing jihad may ironically reintroduce Christians to the prophetic Jesus from whom they have become largely estranged. Muhammad and Jesus waged responsible jihads. Muslims and Christians must as well.

2

The Loss of the Prophetic

Who wants to be well-adjusted to injustice?
What kind of human being do you want to be?

—CORNEL WEST

Christians and Muslims are rapidly losing touch with the prophetic heart of Jesus and Muhammad. This might seem like a controversial statement since, as we will shortly see, examples do exist in both traditions of people speaking up—and more important, speaking out—on many of the most important justice issues of our day: economic inequality; issues of race, gender, and sexual orientation; and global climate change. But while these prophetic voices do exist, they are being increasingly drowned out by an ever growing chorus of culturally accommodationist Muslims and Christians bent on reinterpreting their respective traditions in ways that advance rather than challenge systems of injustice. Authentic prophetic voices are in great danger of disappearing from the contemporary landscape, a reality that could well prove disastrous for the future of life on earth. Christians and Muslims desperately need to reclaim the prophetic heart of the central figures of their respective traditions. But before they can do this they will need to be clear on exactly what the word *prophetic* really means. Let me begin with a definition.

DEFINING PROPHETIC

The term *prophetic*, through its association with words like *prophecy* or *prophet*, is understood by many to be about predicting the future. We think of prophets as people with a special ability to peer into the distant future and discern the unfolding of coming events, especially when the events in question are associated with end-of-the-world scenarios. Like Hal Lindsey and his once wildly popular book *The Late Great Planet Earth*, prophecy is connected today almost exclusively to the kinds of apocalyptic end-time predictions that dominate in popular culture (the best-selling Left Behind series of Christian novels, for example). But this view of prophecy is decidedly modern and represents a conservative Christian corruption that does not accord at all well with the role that prophets normally play in the pages of the Bible.

This conservative Protestant corruption is interesting given how much emphasis conservative Protestants place on Scripture. In the scriptural text, a prophet acts less like a fortuneteller waving her hands over a crystal ball and more like a figure who speaks truth to power (and frequently suffers the consequences). Biblical prophets speak uncomfortable truths to kings and priests, and call nations to account for their ethical lapses and moral failings. To be confronted with a truly prophetic voice is to be made uncomfortable, to be convicted by conscience of one's moral failings. Fortunetellers are a dime a dozen; it is the authentically prophetic voice speaking truth to power that is in great danger of being lost from the contemporary world.

The premier example of a prophetic voice in the pages of the Bible aside from Jesus (whose prophetic career I will discuss in depth in chapter four) is Amos, the lowly shepherd of Tekoa who stood up to the powerful kingdom of Israel in the eighth century BCE. Amos's prophetic career paralleled the reign of King Jeroboam II, a time of great material affluence in the kingdom of Israel. Not only does Amos's portrayal of life in Israel emphasize the great wealth of the kingdom, as we will shortly see, but archaeological evidence enhances this portrait in a dramatic way. Excavations done at the royal palace in Samaria (the capital city of Israel) have turned up dozens of beautifully carved and intricately detailed ivory pieces (dubbed the Samaritan ivories) dated to the reign of King Jeroboam II. Ivory was one of the rarest and most expensive materials available in the ancient world, and if the royal artisans of Israel could use it simply as a medium for their artwork, the kingdom to which Amos was prophetically sent must have been very wealthy indeed. It would be like installing bath fixtures of twenty-four-karat gold!

Amos was not a member of this affluent society. He hailed from the southern kingdom of Judah, and given his occupation, Amos represented about the lowest socioeconomic class recognized by ancient societies: Amos was a shepherd. But God sent this lowly shepherd to the powerful kingdom to the north and empowered him to preach against it. What exactly was the content of Amos's prophecy? Consider the following passages.

Amos begins:

> Thus says the LORD:
> For three transgressions of Israel and for four,
>   I will not revoke the punishment;
> because they sell the righteous for silver
>   and the needy for a pair of sandals—
> they who trample the head of the poor into the dust of the earth,
>   and push the afflicted out of the way. (2:6–7)[1]

Clearly "trickle-down" economics did not work any better in ancient Israel than it has in modern America! The elites of society were hoarding the enormous wealth of this affluent kingdom and exploiting the poor, a situation that in Amos's view did not accord with the dictates of God. This is not a minor key in the book of Amos but the major chord that Amos strikes over and over again.

As the prophecy continues, Amos piles up image after image of a decadent, affluent elite who hold little regard for the poor clawing at their gates. For example, in chapter 4, Amos introduces us to "the cows of Bashan"

> who oppress the poor, who crush the needy,
>   who say to their husbands, "Bring something to drink!" (4:1)

Considering that Bashan was an extremely fertile grazing area on which feeding livestock would become very satisfied, Amos's comparison of Israelite women to fattened cows is not meant as a compliment! These wealthy, self-satisfied women lie around all day without a care in the world, calling to their husbands to wait on them hand and foot while the poor are starving in the streets.

Amos offers another striking image:

> Alas for those who lie on beds of ivory,
>   and lounge on their couches,

1. All biblical quotations are from the New Revised Standard Version.

and eat lambs from the flock
    and calves from the stall;
who sing idle songs to the sound of the harp,
    and like David improvise on instruments of music;
who drink wine from bowls,
    and anoint themselves with the finest oils,
    but are not grieved over the ruins of Joseph!
Therefore they shall now be the first to go into exile,
    and the revelry of the loungers shall pass away. (6:4–7)

Talk about a self-satisfied crowd! Freed from the necessity of work by their vast accumulated wealth, the Israelite elites have nothing better to do than lie around on beds of ivory (recall the Samaritan ivories), drink wine, make music, and stuff themselves on lamb chops, totally unaware that their demise is imminent.

The least they could do is attend church and pray for forgiveness (or do they attend one of those health-and-wealth churches where they are told that God blesses their affluence?), but even this does not work out so well. In the best-known passage in Amos, God castigates the Israelite elite:

I hate, I despise your festivals,
    and I take no delight in your solemn assemblies.
Even though you offer me your burnt offerings and grain offerings,
    I will not accept them;
and the offerings of well-being of your fatted animals
    I will not look upon.
Take away from me the noise of your songs;
    I will not listen to the melody of your harps.
But let justice roll down like waters,
    and righteousness like an ever-flowing stream. (5:21–24)

To summarize, worship means nothing if justice is not being done. The elite can play their harps until their fingers bleed, sing hymns until they are hoarse, and sacrifice everything in their possession, but if they continue to crush the needy for a pair of sandals, God couldn't care less about their worship. Justice is at the heart of Amos's prophetic message. This is the prophetic voice at its best—calling the powerful to account on behalf of the powerless.

The easiest way to fully grasp the truly prophetic spirit of Amos's message is to examine the reaction to his preaching. Do thousands of people flock to his church, enriching Amos and leading him to begin a worldwide television ministry? Not exactly! The priest Amaziah reproaches Amos with the words: "O seer, go, flee away to the land of Judah, earn your bread there, and prophesy there; but never again prophesy at Bethel, for it is the king's sanctuary, and it is a temple of the kingdom" (7:12–13). In other words, "Get out of here, Amos! Take your prophecy and go home." When one exercises an authentically prophetic voice, rejection by the defenders of the unjust status quo will almost always be the result. Prophetic preaching at its best is always disconcerting and may at times be deemed downright objectionable—at least by those who are the targets of the prophetic critique.

With Amos as the paradigm for the prophetic voice at its best, it is easy to survey the history of Christianity and Islam and find numerous other examples of prophetic voices. Of course, Jesus and Muhammad immediately come to mind, but I will deal with them extensively in later chapters. Two modern examples that are hard to ignore are Martin Luther King Jr. and Malcolm X. Neither was out for his own self-aggrandizement. Both experienced rejection and ultimately assassination at the hands of the powers of the status quo. But both effectively spoke truth to power on behalf of the marginalized and oppressed, and they transformed the social dynamics of America in a positive way. Tarek Mehanna has it right. Malcolm X was a *mujahid* (one who wages jihad), and Martin Luther King Jr. was too. And their examples clearly demonstrate one of the reasons why people shy away from exercising their own prophetic voice; doing so can be life-threatening. There is little danger in trying to predict the end of the world, but a true prophetic calling is not for the faint of heart.

Other examples of authentically prophetic voices exist in both Christianity and Islam, and I will briefly mention some of them below. Yet despite the obvious existence of great prophetic figures in both traditions, these prophetic voices are becoming more distant and harder to hear as an increasing number of Christians and Muslims settle into an understanding of their faith that accommodates to systems of injustice rather than resisting them. What is the evidence for this loss of the prophetic? It is all around us.

THE LOSS OF THE PROPHETIC IN CHRISTIANITY

Before documenting the loss of the prophetic in Christianity, let's consider a few examples of the Christian prophetic voice in action in order to throw into stark relief the decidedly nonprophetic forms of Christianity that are coming to dominate today. Coming face-to-face with a truly prophetic voice will emphasize by contrast just how unprophetic the majority of contemporary Christians have become.

One noteworthy example of a Christian prophetic voice was raised in the midst of the 2012 presidential campaign. Republican presidential candidate Mitt Romney chose Wisconsin congressman Paul Ryan as his running mate. Paul Ryan was known for authoring a federal budget proposal that would slash government spending on programs for the poor (like Medicaid and food stamps) while transforming Medicare into a privatized voucher program. This budget proposal, not surprisingly, also reduced taxes on the wealthiest Americans. Paul Ryan's budget proposal, if it were ever enacted, would clearly increase the level of economic injustice in America by shifting greater amounts of wealth upward away from the poor and middle class toward the very wealthy. In response to this unjust budget proposal, the U.S. Conference of Catholic Bishops exercised an authentically prophetic voice by pronouncing immoral the budget proposal of their fellow Catholic. Not to be outdone by the male Catholic hierarchy, a group of nuns under the leadership of Sister Simone Campbell (the Nuns on the Bus) made an extensive bus tour, prophetically exposing the injustice at the heart of Paul Ryan's politically motivated budget proposal. More recently, Pope Francis made a real stir among the wealthy elites of the United States with his prophetic condemnation of wealth inequality and secular capitalist ethics (more on this later). The prophetic voice is still alive in the Roman Catholic Church, at least on the issue of the economy.

Catholics are not alone. The Protestant denomination with which my college is affiliated, the Evangelical Lutheran Church in America, issues social statements on a variety of topics like economic injustice, war and peace, gay rights, and climate change that challenge the unjust status quo and are thus prophetic in their nature. Individual churches in a number of denominations have adopted an open and affirming stance toward homosexuality—a clearly prophetic response to the fortunately waning homophobia of the larger society. Of course, no discussion of the prophetic voice in Christianity would be complete without mention of the prophetic antiwar stance of the peace churches: Quakers and Mennonites. And we can't avoid mentioning Cornel West, the contemporary social critic who has taught at Harvard and Princeton, and who now works at Union Theological Seminary in New York City. West's untiring advocacy in behalf of the victims of racial and economic injustice raises the bar for all of us on what it means to exercise a prophetic voice. The prophetic voice is not dead in Christianity, and in fact the foregoing discussion makes it appear that it is alive and well. But nothing could be further from the truth. These examples all stem from Catholicism and mainline Protestantism, but the influence of both Catholicism and mainline Protestantism is rapidly declining in American society. These islands of the prophetic are being replaced by the explosive surge of the nondenominational evangelical megachurch and its political reflection, the decidedly nonprophetic Religious Right.

Evidence abounds that the prophetic voice still crying out in mainline Christian circles is being drowned out by a growing chorus of conservative evangelical voices so co-opted by the powers of the unjust status quo that among these evangelicals prophetic denunciation of the powers is seen as tantamount to heresy. The television airwaves are filled with entertaining pop-culture preachers selling a health-and-wealth gospel completely accommodated to the corporate-dominated economic system of injustice and exploitation. According to these clergy of capitalist propaganda, God does not denounce increasing levels of wealth inequality and the exploitation of the poor by the rich (as Amos's God does). Rather, God wants you to be rich too. God wants to move you into the class of the exploiters while leaving the system of exploitation itself untouched—that is, if you will just pledge your allegiance (and your money!) to these apostles of greed.

Examples of these health-and-wealth preachers are too numerous to mention in detail. But certainly one of the most influential and entertaining is Joel Osteen, leader of what is reputed to be the largest church in America, the Lakewood Church in Houston, Texas. I say it is reputed to be the largest because apparently Lakewood Church does not keep official membership statistics, so it is unclear just how many people are connected to it. But given that they fill their enormous World Mission Center (the Houston Rockets' old basketball arena) for multiple services every weekend, it is hard to imagine there is a larger church anywhere in the country. Osteen's sermons run on several cable television outlets, his books (with shallow, pop-psychology titles like *Your Best Life Now*) appear on the *New York Times* best-seller list (and are ubiquitous in airport bookstores), and Osteen travels the country presenting "An Evening with Joel and Victoria" (his wife). Joel Osteen's theologically vacuous message of material flourishing truly influences many millions of people.

Perhaps the best measurement of his influence is the regularity with which he appears on high-profile news and entertainment shows. Osteen was a favorite of Larry King's before King retired, and he continued to appear with some regularity on the show that for a while occupied King's CNN time slot—*Piers Morgan Tonight*. No matter how many times Larry King or Piers Morgan tried to get Joel or his wife Victoria to engage a hot political topic where they might possibly exercise a prophetic voice, they consistently refused. Over and over again Joel simply states that he is not a political person; he is just interested in sharing God's love with people. But you don't have to listen very long to realize that for him, God's love is demonstrated in a person's life by how materially successful that person becomes. Osteen's preaching is health and wealth all the way. It reifies the economic status quo; it never challenges it. It's funny that the Nuns on the Bus never seem to get similar levels of exposure on such high-profile broadcasts. Because an authentically prophetic voice makes us uncomfortable, we prefer to ignore it. Joel Osteen tells us what we want to hear, so we flock to his church with little thought to the theological vacuity and moral ambiguity of the message he is selling (and I do mean *selling*, in the strict sense of the word. Olsteen is more salesman than pastor or prophet!).

Gender justice is another issue that gets short shrift in the world of evangelical megachurches. It is, of course, true that recent years have witnessed the rise of several female megachurch media personalities. Joyce Meyer is the most obvious example, with her many best-selling books. But women are still denied ordination in many conservative Protestant churches (and in the Roman Catholic Church too), and, more important, the evangelical world continues to reinforce very traditional patriarchal gender roles within the family. One thinks of the Promise Keepers, an evangelical movement designed to call men back to their "rightful place" as authoritative heads of households. (I know of an evangelical couple that holds gender-segregated Bible studies for college students!) It may be that women are no longer kept barefoot and pregnant (though recent battles over access to contraceptives might lead to that!), but there is little evidence of the Religious Right's advocating for full gender equality as a God-ordained mandate. Women continue to face an uphill battle in the struggle (jihad) for equality of opportunity, and you are not likely to hear many evangelical Christians advocating for issues like paycheck fairness (since this is deemed part of a liberal agenda).

On issues of sexual orientation, some mainline churches are beginning to recognize that all forms of discrimination are antithetical to the gospel, and these are taking prophetic stances in support of gay rights; but the far more influential Christian Right continues its firm antihomosexual stand. Organizations like the Family Research Council and its politically influential leader, Tony Perkins, oppose gay rights and gay marriage with a crusader's zeal. Fortunately they are losing this battle as the larger society is quickly becoming much less homophobic, but the prophetic voices standing in solidarity with the often vilified gay and lesbian community are not coming from the mouths of the politically influential conservative Christian community.

One area in which a Christian prophetic voice is really difficult to hear is that of climate change and environmental injustice. Given that the life-altering and even life-threatening effects of climate change (rising sea levels, severe droughts, and so forth) will be experienced most acutely by those who are least responsible for the problem, climate change is manifestly an issue of justice, and therefore one that must be addressed prophetically. But don't hold your breath. The evangelical Christian movement has had a near stranglehold on this issue. A particularly useful video clip available on YouTube shows Illinois congressman John Shimkus testifying several years ago at a congressional subcommittee hearing on climate change. To support his claim that climate change is not an issue of concern, Shimkus opens a Bible to the book of Genesis, reads the passage from the Noah story where God pledges to never again destroy the earth by a flood, and then closes the Bible, emphasizing his belief in the Bible as the infallible word of God. Since God says he will never again destroy the earth by a flood, Shimkus concludes that the dangerous sea-level rises associated with climate change will not occur. End of story.[2] This would be humorous if not so tragic. Shimkus's denial of climate change has a long legacy in the marriage between aspects of the Religious Right and the Republican Party.

This marriage is well documented by Stephanie Hendricks, an Emmy-winning broadcast journalist and author of *Divine Destruction: Wise Use, Dominion Theology, and the Making of American Environmental Policy*. According to Hendricks, the term *wise use* was originally coined by President Theodore Roosevelt's U.S. Forest Services head, Gifford Pinchot, in 1903. Pinchot coined this term to describe his belief that a balance had to be struck between taking care of the forests and the interests of an expanding human population. For Pinchot, wilderness lands were to be used, but

---

2. *American Clean Energy Security Act: Hearing on Preparing for Climate Change: Adaptation Policies and Programs: Hearing on H.R. 2454, Before the Subcommittee on Energy and Environment, 111th Cong. March 25, 2009* (statement of John Shimkus, Republican representative from Illinois). YouTube video, 2:25. Posted March 27, 2009, by Progress Illinois, https://www.youtube.com/watch?v=_7h08RDYA5E/.

used wisely. In the 1980s and 1990s, however, a new wise-use movement developed that fundamentally altered Pinchot's view to say that humans have a right to the use of all natural resources with little concern for the long term sustainability of those resources. According to the guru of the modern wise-use movement, Bill Arnold, "Our limitless imaginations can break through natural limits to make earthly goods and carrying capacity virtually infinite."[3]

More problematic, however, is the wedding of this modern antienvironmental wise-use doctrine to a particular strain of evangelical Christian thought dubbed "dominion theology." Dominionists believe that God has bestowed on humanity the privilege of exercising complete control and dominion over God's creation, to exercise that dominion in whatever way they see fit. Oftentimes dominion theology is interpreted through the lens of apocalyptic, end-times scenarios raising the specter that Jesus will not return to earth until the earth's natural resources have been exhausted. In fact some believe it is incumbent upon Christians to exhaust those resources as quickly as possible as a way of hastening Jesus's return! But most disturbing of all, Hendricks meticulously documents the extent to which high-level government officials during the presidency of George W. Bush subscribed to these wise-use and dominionist ideas—including President Bush himself! These Christian theological ideas drove environmental policy in a decidedly antienvironmental direction. Evangelical Christianity has totally failed in its prophetic calling and we are now paying a steep price. We may be reaching the point of no return in disastrous climate change.

Not only have conservative Christians helped drive antienvironmental political policies, they have in recent years walked in lockstep with conservative political movements on issues of economic policy. As wealth inequality in America has ballooned over the last thirty or so years in large part due to tax policies that shift wealth from the poor and middle class upward to the wealthy, evangelical Christians have become almost entirely identified with the political party that has authorized these policies. Through Ralph Reed's Christian Coalition, the aforementioned Tony Perkins's Family Research Council, the late Jerry Falwell's Moral Majority, and movements spawned by Pat Robertson, conservative Christians have been marshaled into a vast politically powerful ally of the Republican Party and its regressive economic policies that have exacerbated the kinds of economic injustice that would send the prophet Amos into an apoplectic fit.

3. Hendricks, *Divine Destruction*, 31.

The Christian prophetic voice on economic issues has been almost entirely drowned out.

One more way that evangelical Christians have completely abdicated any kind of prophetic vocation is in their unbridled support for Israel at the expense of the Palestinian people. Of course the Israeli/Palestinian issue is a complex one, and forces on both sides undermine efforts to achieve a lasting and just peace. But to hear the Christian Zionists tell it, God has bestowed on Israel all rights to this land, and the Palestinian people are merely an impediment to Israel's fulfillment of a divine promise (they play the role played by the unfortunate Canaanites in the Joshua conquest narrative in the Bible). In this view, the growth of illegal Israeli settlements and the injustices these perpetrate on largely defenseless Palestinian citizens is of no concern. This land belongs to Israel and only to Israel. God ordained it. Period! With this unfettered evangelical Christian support for all things Israel, one will never hear a prophetic denunciation of Israel's heavy-handed military tactics issuing from the lips of your average evangelical.

In the midst of all this Christian accommodation to systems of injustice, ordinary Christians themselves have completely given up their prophetic vocation by adhering to a depoliticized version of Christian faith that emphasizes personal piety over all else. I frequently surprise the students I teach by telling them they practice a form of narcissistic faith. Their faith is all about them. It's "Jesus loves *me*; this I know; for the Bible tells *me* so." Their faith is something very personal that helps them in their lives but rarely challenges them to open up to larger structural questions. I also explain to them that their tendency toward narcissistic faith is not really their fault. They have been raised in an increasingly narcissistic society that emphasizes personal, material success and fulfillment over all else. Of course they are narcissistic. How could it be otherwise! Where Christian faith becomes nothing more than the development of personal piety, the prophetic voice is effectively silenced.

The prophetic voice is not entirely missing from American Christianity. If one listens closely, one can still hear its faint echoes. But those echoes are being drowned out by the loud chorus of a culturally accommodationist, pietistic Christianity that threatens the last vestiges of an authentically Christian prophetic message, and the country and the world are the worse off for it. Reversing this situation will not be easy and unfortunately might well prove to be impossible. But there is at least a glimmer of hope that Christians can rekindle the fire of their prophetic heart, and, ironically, learning to engage the Islamic concept of jihad might just be the necessary prescription to make this happen. Muslims have something important to teach Christians—that is, if Muslims can authentically engage jihad themselves. Unfortunately, the prophetic voice is growing fainter among Muslims too, and the Islamophobic spirit of our times is increasingly forcing most Muslims to back away from a full-throated embrace of the prophetic spirit of jihad. Let's consider the situation of Islam in more detail.

THE LOSS OF THE PROPHETIC IN ISLAM

Just as the Christian prophetic voice has not been utterly silenced, so the Muslim prophetic voice has not entirely disappeared, and it will be useful to consider a few examples of its continuing activity in order to create a contrast with the growing dominance of nonprophetic forms of Islam. Since the publication of my 2009 book, *Was Jesus a Muslim? Questioning Categories in the Study of Religion*, I have developed a close working relationship with the Islamic Organization of North America, or IONA for short. Headquartered in suburban Detroit, IONA is a relatively small network of North American Muslims dedicated to a nonviolent struggle to bring about the just and equitable society they believe is ordained by God in the Qur'an. The members of IONA understand Islam not primarily as a confessional religious identity but as an orientation toward a life of submission to God that issues in the call to work for justice and peace. IONA is very much a prophetic organization, and I have thoroughly enjoyed the privilege of interacting with its members and sharing a Christian prophetic perspective on issues of politics and economics—a perspective that coheres very closely with theirs. IONA grew out of the work of an extraordinary individual in Pakistan, Israr Ahmad, who stands as a prime example of the prophetic voice in twentieth- and twenty-first-century Islam. I will engage the work of Israr Ahmad in more detail in a later chapter.

Another contemporary scholar of note is Tariq Ramadan. Ramadan is a Swiss-born Muslim who specializes in articulating a specifically Western European form of Islam. This does not mean, however, that Ramadan advocates a form of Islam that simply accommodates to Western cultural norms. Rather, in books titled *Western Muslims and the Future of Islam* and *Radical Reform*, he advocates for an Islam that challenges and resists the worst aspects of Western culture, especially its thorough involvement in the exploitative systems of global capitalism. Ramadan's is a truly prophetic voice, a point underscored by his being banned from the United States some years ago despite having been invited to occupy an endowed chair in peace studies at the University of Notre Dame. Shortly before Ramadan was to leave Switzerland for South Bend, Indiana, his visa was revoked by the Department of Homeland Security with little explanation as to why. For one thing, Ramadan happens to be the grandson of Hasan al-Banna, the founder of the Muslim Brotherhood in Egypt, which at the time of Ramadan's banning was considered a terrorist organization by the U.S. government. (Later it would become the duly elected—and quickly overthrown—government of Egypt. How times change!) For another thing, Ramadan has never shied away from prophetically challenging Western policies toward the so-called Muslim world. Given these two things, his banning (which was later reversed) is not entirely surprising. Prophetic Muslims make Americans nervous, which is the primary reason that Tarek Mehanna is in jail.

Another important contemporary figure is Mahmoud Mohamed Taha, a Sudanese scholar executed by the Sudanese Islamic government in 1985 for advocating strongly in favor of the expansion of civil, political, and economic equality for all people through a rather radical reinterpretation of shariah (traditional Islamic law). Taha contended in his book *The Second Message of Islam* that the later revelations of the Qur'an, which contain much of the traditional legal material that informs shariah, are provisional and were revealed only to assist Muslims in developing to a point where they could fully embrace the grand egalitarian vision contained in the earlier revelations. This creative and bold reinterpretation of the authority of the Qur'an—essentially rendering more than half of the Muslim scriptures to provisional status in the interest of promoting justice within Sudanese society—was too much for the traditional Muslim government. But Taha nevertheless stands as a true mark of the prophetic voice.

Farid Esack, a contemporary South African Islamic scholar, is another prime example of an Islamic prophetic voice. Esack grew up under the influence of the racial apartheid system in South Africa, an experience that firmly crystallized in his mind that resisting oppressive structures had to be a fundamental aspect of what it means to be a Muslim. Today, Esack describes himself as a postmodern, feminist, liberationist Muslim, and he has actively spoken out against the ravages of the corporate-dominated, global capitalist world, which lead to the exploitation of large sectors of the world's population.

Sometimes a prophetic voice emerges in a most unexpected form. In October of 2012, a member of the Taliban shot a fifteen-year-old Pakistani girl in the head as she walked home from school. Why? Because from the time she was eleven, she had been advocating for the right of girls to be educated. Malala Yousafzai's story quickly spread around the world, resulting in her winning the Nobel Peace Prize in 2014. Having now miraculously recovered from her injuries, she continues with her educational activism despite the severe physical and emotional trauma it caused her and the continuing danger to her life. Her courage is an inspiration to all and an example of the kinds of prophetic activism possible in the contemporary world. One need not be an experienced social activist; one need only have the courage to stand up for what is right. This beautiful Pakistani girl should give us all pause as we look in the mirror and wonder what has happened to our own prophetic voice.

Given that it runs in the same vein as Malala Yousafzai's mission, I must note the work of 2003 Nobel Peace Prize laureate Shirin Ebadi, the Iranian human-rights activist who has run afoul of the Iranian regime, been imprisoned, had her Peace Prize confiscated, and who now must live in exile from her beloved homeland. In 2011 Ebadi spoke at Luther College, and I was privileged to drive her back to the airport after her lecture. She was heading from Luther directly to Geneva, Switzerland, for a major United Nations human-rights conference to present evidence of human-rights violations in Iran. Alas, her flight from La Crosse, Wisconsin, to Chicago was canceled, necessitating that we jump back in the car to drive from La Crosse to Minneapolis to catch another flight to Geneva—and with little time to spare. After three hours of driving I got her to Minneapolis on time (without incurring a speeding ticket!). But the whole way, she was more concerned with the fact that she was inconveniencing *me* than with anything else, repeatedly expressing concern about my having to drive home alone from Minneapolis in the middle of the night. (I actually made it home by midnight.) The depth of her humanity was truly touching and something I will never forget. But clearly it is that depth of humanity along with a tremendous wellspring of courage that makes it possible for her to stand strong against the Iranian regime in defense of its victims. What an inspiration she is—and was—to the students of Luther College!

There are many other Muslim scholars and activists who could be recognized as living their faith in an authentically prophetic way. Hamid Dabashi has authored an entire book on Islamic liberation theology. Imam

Daayiee Abdullah founded the Light of Reform mosque in Washington DC, one of the first mosques in the country openly supportive of gay and lesbian people. But these names stand out as noteworthy for the simple reason that they seem to be the exception rather than the rule. By and large as one looks around the world, it is becoming harder and harder to perceive a prophetic Islam at work in the midst of all the Islamic monarchies, dictatorships, and medieval tribal societies that command the majority of our attention.

Gender injustice is, of course, a favorite topic of discussion among the many critics of Islam. Islam is accused of being inherently misogynistic since women are forced to cover their heads or even their entire bodies; they are denied education, the right to drive, and the right to work outside the home; and they are subject to various forms of violence, the worst perhaps being honor killings or the disfigurement of those accused of violating standards of honor. Now, the status of women in Islamic societies is much more complex than these stereotypes portray. Many Muslim women are well educated, work as doctors and university professors, serve as heads of state, and live within caring and supportive family units. (It should not pass unnoticed that Muslim-majority countries have elected at least five women as heads of state while the U.S. still awaits its first.) But misogynistic practices unfortunately do occur in Islamic societies at a level that we cannot ignore. Stonings of women accused of adultery still occur in some Muslim countries—even where stoning is officially outlawed. Gender injustice is a significant issue for Muslims and has prompted the American Muslim convert Amina Wadud to declare, through the title of one of her books, a "gender jihad."[4]

Religious intolerance is another issue plaguing a number of Muslim countries. In medieval Spain, Jews, Christians, and Muslims lived in relative peace and harmony under the auspices of an Islamic government. But religious minorities today find it difficult to gain respect in places like Saudi Arabia, Afghanistan, Pakistan, Iran, and Nigeria. Just ask the Coptic Christians in Egypt how well they are respected! And now we have the depraved ugliness of ISIS to contend with in Syria and Iraq. Along with religious intolerance, gratuitous violence is an all too common occurrence in Muslim countries. Sometimes this violence is directed at non-Muslim enemies, whether real or perceived (America, Israel); at other times, violence is directed at fellow Muslims, especially in conflicts between Sunni and Shi'ite

4. Wadud, *Inside the Gender Jihad.*

Muslims. The issue of violence goes well beyond just al-Qaeda and other so-called terrorist organizations.

The unjust nature of Muslim-induced violence was brought home in a big way in September 2012 when the United States Consulate in Benghazi, Libya, was attacked and ambassador Chris Stevens and three other U.S. diplomatic personnel were killed. Chris Stevens was well liked and respected by many Libyans. But this attack was supposed to be retaliation for the release of an American movie painting a very disparaging portrait of the Prophet Muhammad. Soon, protests against this movie, some of whom turned violent, broke out at U.S. embassies in more than a dozen Muslim countries, despite the repeated (true) assertion that the U.S. government had nothing to do with the movie. Ambassador Stevens and his colleagues did not deserve to die. This assassination was carried out by Muslims who demonstrate a complete disconnect from an authentically prophetic heart central to the Islamic tradition.

The existence of Islam-sponsored violence and injustice is really rather incongruous; the Islamic message is wholly opposed to such activities! A little historical perspective will help illustrate this. Before the advent of Islam in seventh-century Arabia, Arab society was tribal and was built upon an honor/shame system of ethics. In a tribal society, a person's individual identity is subordinate to their tribal and clan identities. Primary loyalty is to tribe and clan, and the chief purpose of life is to maintain the honor of one's tribe and clan. Any activity by one tribe that is seen to dishonor another must be met with retaliation in order to restore the lost honor. Because of this system, pre-Islamic society was characterized by escalating blood feuds and so with gratuitous violence.

Into this environment the Islamic message was born, with its call to replace loyalty to tribe and clan with loyalty and submission to a single all-embracing deity—Allah. This call for submission to a unified God implied the unity of humanity in submission to this one God, an idea expressed by the Islamic concept of the Ummah (the worldwide Muslim community), an idea designed to heal the fractures of a tribal world: God is one, and people are one. The tribal honor/shame system was superseded by a new message of submission to one God and to an ethic of mercy and compassion expressed by the constantly repeated phrase "In the name of God, the merciful, the compassionate." In fact, after the early Muslim movement had defeated the members of the Quraysh tribe who resisted the Islamic message, Muhammad led his victorious group of followers to Mecca, where the population, still living according to tribal politics, fully expected Muhammad to exact a terrible and bloody revenge. He would have been justified in doing so, given that many members of his group had been killed by the Quraysh, and given that the honor/shame system demanded retaliation to restore lost honor. But Muhammad did not order the anticipated bloodbath. He served notice with his actions that the tribal honor/shame system was totally antithetical to the new vision of peace and justice embodied in the Islamic message.

Given this, I am struck by how tenacious the old tribalism is, surviving right up to contemporary times even in places where people unanimously label themselves Muslim! One only has to look at the Taliban in Afghanistan and Pakistan to see the old tribalism at work in a Muslim guise, as witnessed by the barbaric retaliatory attack in December 2014 on the military school in Peshawar that killed more than one hundred children. Or the attack on the French satirical magazine *Charlie Hebdo* in January 2015 meant to avenge cartoons denigrating Muhammad. The violent protests directed at U.S. embassies in retaliation for a movie disparaging Muhammad are entirely explainable as a reflex of this old tribalism still at work. Muhammad has been dishonored. Honor must be restored via retaliation aimed at any and all members of the offending tribe (in this case, the Americans). In an honor/shame system, retaliation does not have to be directed at the offending individual; it can be aimed at any member of the offending tribe since individual identity is subordinated to group identity. American embassy workers simply became targets of convenience in this tribal retaliatory system that makes a mockery of Islamic values.

Honor killings of women accused of bringing dishonor on their families is another obvious example of how the old tribal system is still deeply entrenched in places where the Islamic message should have transcended it—but unfortunately has not. The reasons for this failure are complex and beyond the scope of this book. But such complexity is a reminder of the distance separating the Islamic message of justice and peace from the lives of those perpetrating injustice under a Muslim guise. Muslims are in just as much need as Christians are when it comes to reclaiming their prophetic voice.

No discussion of the loss of the prophetic in Islam would be complete without some comment on the issue of economics. Muslim countries have been rife with all sorts of economic injustices due to the corrupt dictatorships and monarchies by which they have been ruled. It is another great irony of Muslim history that Muslim countries have been so often ruled by kings and dictators when you realize that these forms of government are antithetical to the basic principles of Islamic teachings. The early Muslim movement (at least the majority-Sunni movement) was led by a series of caliphs whose authority to lead was based on consultation with and the consensus of the community—an early form of democracy, if you will. But quickly this early movement was transformed into a hereditary monarchy with the emergence of the Umayyad Dynasty in 661 CE, and Muslim lands have frequently been ruled historically by dynasties and more recently by corrupt dictatorships—dictatorships often propped up by Western colonial powers for their own imperial interests. In this situation, wealth has been hoarded by an elite class at the expense of the majority of the citizens of Muslim lands creating an unjust economic system totally at odds with the vision of justice and equality at the heart of the Islamic message. Deposed Egyptian dictator Hosni Mubarak, for example, is estimated to have amassed a fortune of at least $5 billion while ruling over a country with enormous levels of unemployment and poverty.

One final way the prophetic voice is disappearing from Islam is through the growing emphasis on personal piety so characteristic of the modern, individualistic world. For so many Muslims today, Islam has become simply a personal identity marked by attending regular Islamic rituals, by wearing particular kinds of clothes, or by keeping a distinctive personal appearance. Many Muslim men see it as a sign of piety to grow a beard as a way to imitate Muhammad, for example. For others, being Muslim is defined by nothing more than performing the Five Pillars of Islam with little critical reflection on what those pillars actually mean.

Several years ago I had the privilege to travel to the Muslim Community Association of South Bay in the Silicon Valley area of California. This is a very large Islamic center where thousands of Muslims gather every Friday for prayer. I went there with the emir of IONA, Mustapha Elturk, to speak on my earlier book, *Was Jesus a Muslim?* Since we were there for the Friday prayers, Emir Mustapha was invited to deliver the *khutbah* (short sermon) during the service. He addressed the Five Pillars of Islam and asked the gathered worshipers a very important question: What are pillars for? Pillars, we know, are support structures. They are the foundation of a building but not coeval with the building itself. Emir Mustapha employed this analogy to argue that the Five Pillars of Islam cannot be understood as the whole of Islam. They are mere supports that hold up a larger edifice.

Islam is the superstructure that rests on the pillars—the complete and total structure for all aspects of life, including political and economic affairs. At the conclusion of the *khutbah*, one of the worshipers approached Emir Mustapha visibly upset with his remarks. This person could not come to grips with the idea that his regular engagement with the Five Pillars by itself did not make him a Muslim. The call to prophetically confront the world and engage the struggle for justice was very threatening to him. (Remember that this is a very affluent community of professionals living in Silicon Valley!) The desire for the safe harbor of personal piety completely trumped the call to accept responsibility for the more dangerous activity of advocating for social transformation.

Examples like this abound. Recently I received in the mail a booklet published by a well-meaning Muslim scholar claiming to prove that the name Muhammad appears in the Hebrew text of the Bible in the Song of Solomon 5:16:

> His speech is most sweet,
> and he is altogether desirable.
> This is my beloved and this is my friend . . .

The booklet argues that the Hebrew word rendered "desirable" (*mahamdim*) is actually the proper name Muhammad. According to this argument, the text should read as follows:

> His speech is most sweet,
> and he is Muhammad.
> This is my beloved and this is my friend . . .

This rather fanciful reconstruction just demonstrates how focused so many Muslims have become on minor issues of identity and piety while ignoring the bigger issues of justice and peace. Whether Muhammad is truly referenced or not in the pages of the Bible (and as a biblical scholar, I can say for certain that he isn't) is irrelevant to the issues of social transformation so crucial to Muslim identity and expressed in the concept of jihad. Finding Muhammad in the Bible does not feed a single starving person! But Muslims, unfortunately, are a lot like Christians in this regard. The prophetic voice gets easily drowned out by the modern emphasis on individualized faith, religious identity, and the desire to prove the superiority of one religious system over another. Apologetics are a deadly poison to the prophetic voice.

Perhaps no one exemplifies the great popularity of this apologetic Islam better than Dr. Zakir Naik, an Indian-born medical doctor who now devotes himself full time to public speaking with a view to establishing the superiority of Islam over all other religions. He has become enormously popular in the Muslim world, and one can find dozens of videos of him on YouTube debating Christian and Hindu critics of Islam and systematically undermining their critiques with supposedly impeccable logic as he convinces these critics to convert to Islam. In one rather humorous clip, he "proves" the superiority of the Qur'an over the Bible with the curious claim that the Bible wrongly says that the moon shines with its own light (Gen 1:16–19) while the Qur'an correctly proclaims that the moon shines from reflected light (Surah 25:61). Neither text comments on the source of the moon's light, as far as I can tell, but this example does illuminate the sorry state to which so much Muslim discourse has fallen. This Muslim apologetic discourse would be humorous if it were not so tragic. For Dr. Naik, proving the superiority of Islam seems to be all that matters. The prophetic cry for justice never emanates from his lips.

Even Muslims who do not get caught up in the concerns of individual piety still have good reason to downplay the role of authentic jihad in their worldview because of the Islamophobic environment dominating the West. As jihad and Islam in general become equated with violence and terrorism it is almost impossible for a Muslim of strong prophetic conscience to engage in acts of resistance to injustice, especially injustices authorized by the economic status quo. Consider, for example, the MyJihad Campaign, an effort (and an organization) dedicated to reclaiming jihad from its negative, Islamophobic stereotypes by reinterpreting it as simply a personal struggle to lose weight, stay fit, or make friends with those who are different.[5] These are all good things, but the MyJihad Campaign cheapens the original idea of jihad as the enduring (and dangerous) struggle for social justice and peace. Individualized reinterpretations of jihad are not surprising, however. It is dangerous these days just being a Muslim, not to mention being a Muslim who criticizes global capitalism and free-market fundamentalism, or who takes even nonviolent actions against them. Islamophobia effectively pacifies Muslim prophetic activity, which may well be one of Islamophobia's primary purposes. This is a tragic loss for us all.

So the picture is quite clear. The prophetic voice, while not entirely absent from Christianity and Islam, is becoming increasingly difficult to

5. See http://www.myjihad.org/.

hear. But demonstrating that something *is* the case does not automatically inform us of *why* it is the case. What has led to this loss of the prophetic? Ironically, this loss can be traced directly to the very process that has turned Christianity and Islam themselves into religions in the first place—the process of secularization. Prepare to have the fundamental conceptual categories of the deeply entrenched Western worldview disturbed in this next section. This will be the most theoretically difficult—but perhaps also the most important—part of this book's argument to fully grasp. I therefore beg the reader's patience as we wade into waters where even some seasoned religion scholars are hesitant to go.

SECULARIZATION AND THE LOSS OF THE PROPHETIC

Recent years have witnessed the publication of a spate of new books bearing peculiar titles. For example, in 2005 a scholar of European intellectual history at the University of Michigan, Tomoko Masuzawa, published *The Invention of World Religions*. Leora Batnitzky, a scholar of Jewish thought at Princeton University, has published *How Judaism Became a Religion*. More recently, a book appeared with the title *The Invention of Religion in Japan*. What is peculiar about these titles? As the underlined words show, they all suggest that religion—both in its generic sense and in its particular forms (Judaism)—is something invented, not something real that has always existed at all times and in all places. These titles and others like them alert us to a seismic shift taking place within the academic study of religion whereby an increasing number of scholars now view religion as a human cultural creation, not a fixed real feature of the universe. This truly does represent a sea change in the way religion is understood, and one admittedly so quixotic to the average reader that there may be a real temptation to ignore this idea or pass it off as a simple word game.

Doing so would be a big mistake, however, for recognizing the artificial nature of this generic thing we call "religion" will be a critical move in any attempt to reclaim a truly prophetic heart. It turns out that viewing religion as a real feature of the universe contributes greatly to the silencing of the prophetic voice. Ironically, the more religious we become, the less prophetic we will be! I recognize this is counterintuitive, so let me try to clarify this seemingly bizarre statement.

The prevailing attitude in the West conceives of religion as a defining feature of humanity; we tend to believe that all people throughout history have practiced some form of religion. But since religion in its generic sense is an abstraction—you cannot directly observe it: we say that religion comes in a variety of concrete forms. There are the religions of the ancient world, the religions of indigenous peoples, and the great religions of the modern world like Christianity, Judaism, Islam, Hinduism, Buddhism, and others. In all these cases, religion is considered to be an entity with a clear and distinct essence all its own, which can be clearly distinguished from things that are not considered to be religion—like politics, economics, and science, for example. These distinctions allow us to talk about the relationship between religion and politics or religion and science as if religion, politics, and science are clear and distinct entities. We tend to carve up reality into these discrete realms; then we assume that all people conceive the world in the same way. But these assumptions turn out to be nothing more than manifestations of our Western cultural bias: we assume that all people everywhere think just like we do. But they don't, showing our biases to be culturally imperialistic bravado.

There is no evidence, for example, that ancient peoples recognized a conceptual category called religion understood to be clearly distinct from other aspects of life.[6] Neither the Greek of the New Testament nor the Hebrew of the Old Testament even contains a word equivalent to our English word *religion*. The same is true of the Arabic of the Qur'an. Religion as a distinct concept seems to be missing from indigenous cultures around the world and even in much of Asia. Obviously, if a book can be written with the title *The Invention of Religion in Japan*, there must have been a time in Japan when religion did not yet exist—a time prior to its invention. Scholars are increasingly coming to see that the conceptual category religion conceived as an entity clearly distinct from things like politics and economics is a modern Western (and primarily Christian) invention. Most people throughout history have conceived of the world as an integrated whole where the activity of God or the gods was understood to influence both private and public spheres of life, not just an individual's personal spirituality as we tend to think today. It is really amazing how long it has taken to realize this. Just read the Bible. What does God do other than lead his people in war, anoint and depose kings, criticize economic injustice,

6. See, e.g., Malina, "'Religion' in the World of Paul"; Mason, "Jews, Judeans, Judaizing, Judaism."

and generally meddle in Israel's political affairs in a way that our modern doctrine of separation of church and state would never allow? The cordoning off of the influence of God or the gods into a separate spiritual realm called religion where this influence is understood to be relevant primarily for an individual's faith life has the effect of removing spiritual influence from the political and economic affairs of life. Such removal is what we call the process of secularization.

In his important book *A Secular Age*, philosopher Charles Taylor provides a fascinating account of the changes that have occurred in Western society over the last five hundred years to produce our modern secular world. Taylor observes that five hundred years ago it was virtually impossible not to believe in God. God was thoroughly infused in all aspects of life, and to deny the existence of God did not appear to be a viable option for most people. Any who did question the existence of God were quickly marginalized and branded as heretics (and may have even been burned at the stake!). But today, Taylor argues, belief in God has become a choice, with nonbelief or atheism becoming a perfectly acceptable alternative to belief for a growing number of people. This shift toward the viability of unbelief is for Taylor one of the hallmarks of our secular age.

As unbelief becomes a viable option, Taylor argues that all human experience—including what we might term religious experience—is reframed as deriving entirely from things found within the material realm, and human material flourishing rises to become the highest goal of human existence. To grasp what Taylor is saying, consider the way religious experience is being reframed today by cognitive scientists. Experiments are being done to demonstrate that spiritual impulses and experiences derive entirely from the workings of the material brain. Some have gone so far as to propose the existence of a "God gene" to explain how the religious impulse is simply the result of a materialistic evolutionary process.[7] Belief in God rendered early humans more fit for survival, the theory goes, so belief in God was selected for and passed down to succeeding generations. It is becoming harder and harder for people to believe that their spiritual experiences may actually be the result of authentic connection to a higher spiritual power. Once the experience of spiritual connection is explained away as merely the side effect of physical processes, what is left? Nothing but inanimate matter and energy. This materialistic reframing of all experience is for Taylor the chief characteristic of our secular age.

7. Hamer, *God Gene*; Newberg et al., *Why God Won't Go Away*

As authentic belief in God or the gods fades from view and the influence of transcendent power is removed from the material affairs of life, a separate and distinct realm of human experience called religion is invented to create a safe place to enact moral and ethical norms like justice and compassion, which flow from a transcendent view of reality. Once they are cordoned off into this distinct realm called religion, such moral and ethical norms cannot directly influence the material affairs of life where they might disrupt the secular drive toward competition and material acquisition so characteristic of our secular age. Please don't miss the deep irony that it is the very process of secularization that *creates* the concept of religion! Religion and the secular are codependent terms such that neither has any real meaning apart from the other. Religion is invented as the antithesis of the secular realm, deriving its meaning simply by virtue of what it isn't. That is, religion is understood as that which is not secular; the secular as that which is not religious. Ironically, then, the more secular our society becomes, the more religious it becomes at the same time! Or said another way, the flourishing religiosity of American society is proof of its secularity! What seems like a paradox is no paradox at all. This codependence of religion and the secular is an insight with far-reaching implications for the creation and perpetuation of unjust economic systems. But before we get to this, let me provide a little thought experiment to help illustrate this admittedly abstract codependency principle.

Suppose you lived in a world where everything was blue. Not only was the sky its familiar shade of azure, but so were the trees, the grass, your house, your body—everything. Your world would be thoroughly monochromatic. In such a world, would it ever make sense to use the adjective *blue*? How would the phrase "the blue house" mean anything different from simply saying "the house"? If every house is blue, a phrase like "the blue house" has no referential value. It does not select out a particular color of house from houses of other colors, since there are no red or green or brown houses in this monochromatic world to provide the contrast that gives the word *blue* its meaning. The concept blue would, therefore, be meaningless, and the word would likely not even exist. While the denizens of such a hypothetical world would obviously have the same subjective experience of seeing blue as we do (indeed they would have that experience every waking hour of every day and at night in their dreams!), they would not recognize this experience as the unique experience of seeing blue absent any differing experience to form a contrast with it. In a world where everything is blue, in a very real sense nothing is blue. Things just are what they are.

Likewise, in a world where spiritual experience was encountered in every aspect of life, contemporary words like *religion* and *religious* would have no meanings. The term *religious experience* would have no referential value since all experience would have the character that we describe as religious. Just as the color blue would not be recognized as blue in a monochromatic world, it would be impossible to label any experience as specifically religious in a world where every experience has the quality that we associate with the word *religious*. The experiences *we* describe as religious or spiritual would be simply the constant experience of life for people in a religionless world. The word *religion* only takes on meaning when a new conceptual space called the secular opens up to form its contrast, just as the word *blue* only takes on meaning in the context of a multicolored world. Neither the term *religious* nor the term *secular* carries an independent meaning. Each derives its meaning entirely from its contrast with the other term.

This is not just a word game. These fundamental conceptual structures have a profound influence on the kind of world we create for ourselves. For example, religion scholar Timothy Fitzgerald argues that the invention of a distinct realm called religion is fundamental to the development of the global capitalist economic system. And it should not be hard to see why. In Fitzgerald's view, once the spiritual and moral traditions of humanity get split off and assigned to a separate, religious realm, what is left is a secular realm that appears to be a realm of objective facts—the brute reality of the world as it is rather than as it ought to be. Clearly, once moral values are assigned to the box called religion, the leftover secular landscape must be a neutral ground of objective fact—things simply as they are. But Fitzgerald does not buy this divorcing of values from facts as a neutral description of reality. He believes that the secular world of "facts" is really itself a realm of values too. It is just that when we conceptually assign moral values to the box called religion, it has the *effect* of making the resulting secular landscape *appear* as if it is a realm of objective facts. Herein lies one of the principle roots of economic injustice.

Let's see if we can make this more concrete. Whenever I discuss Fitzgerald's ideas with my students, I always ask them why it is that our economic system is based on the principles of self-interest, competition, and the accumulation of material wealth rather than on the principles of cooperation, mutual caring, and the pursuit of spiritual depth. They usually respond that the question seems absurd. When I press them further as to why, they profess their desire for an economic system organized around the principles of mutual caring and the pursuit of spiritual depth, but they just don't think such a system would be practical because it seems to fly in the face of human nature. Humans are greedy, they say, and so it would be impossible for them to live in an economic system that required them to share their resources rather than to engage in ruthless competition and to feed the desire for unfettered wealth accumulation. Remember the saying, he who has the most toys at the end wins!

My students have bought into the rhetorical structure outlined by Fitzgerald hook, line, and sinker. When moral values like fairness and equality get tucked away in the box called religion, Fitzgerald says, they become "objects of nostalgia."[8] That is, they sound nice but they don't seem to be very practical. This is precisely the response I get from my students when they say that values like sharing and compassion work against the inherent greediness of human nature. Now, since values have been placed in the realm of religion, the leftover secular landscape is conceived as being a value-free space of objective facts. Bingo! This is exactly what my students are saying when they argue that humans are greedy by nature. Greed, they believe, is an objective fact, and so the only practical economic system will be one that can marshal individual greed in a productive way for the benefit of all. And what kind of economic system can do this? Well, it just so happens that this is the capitalist economic theory of Adam Smith in its most fundamental form: humans are rational actors who work to maximize their own self-interest, and as they do so, the invisible hand of the market marshals this self-interested activity so that it works to the benefit of society as a whole.

But is this really how capitalism works? And is it the case that humans are in fact greedy by nature (and always rational for that matter)? As long as one buys into the rhetorical structure as outlined by Fitzgerald, these questions cannot be asked. One cannot question facts! One can only question values. Fitzgerald, for one, does not buy into this rhetorical structure. In his view, principles like self-interest, competition, and the greedy drive for wealth accumulation are not objective facts; they are just as much value statements as the ideas of fairness, equality, and mutual caring. But because they are treated as facts by the vast majority of people, they are not questioned, and this leaves the global capitalist economic system free to impose

8. Fitzgerald, *Ideology of Religious Studies*, 8.

its alternative value system (disguised as fact) on the world, and this imposition leads to the kinds of wealth inequality, exploitation, and injustice that we are far too familiar with today.

Now, how does all this explain the loss of the prophetic in Christianity and Islam? The invention of religion conceived as an entity distinct from the secular realm of politics and economics leaves most Christians and an increasing number of Muslims to view their respective traditions primarily as spiritual traditions with little relevance for political and economic affairs. Christians become so focused on issues like individual sin and salvation that the mere suggestion that Jesus's primary mission might have been one of prophetic resistance to the political and economic injustices of his day is tantamount to heresy. As the saying goes, Christians are so heavenly minded that they are no earthly good! For their part, Muslims get so caught up in performing the Five Pillars and defending all the cultural trappings associated with Islam (for instance, particular types of dress, particular foods, beards for men, veils for women) that the idea of Muhammad as a prophetic resistor to the injustices of seventh-century Arabia falls on deaf ears. The very act of raising a prophetic voice against contemporary issues of economic injustice gets vilified as the abuse of religion for political ends. Church and state (or mosque and state) must be kept separate, we are told.

As Christians and Muslims retreat into a world of individualistic piety, cowed into prophetic submission by the deeply rooted religious/secular divide, the motivation to raise a voice of prophetic challenge to the systems of injustice we see all around us quickly dissipates. As long as Christians and Muslims can go about the business of fulfilling the pietistic dictates of their respective traditions, there is no need to engage the political mandates of their founders, and it may even be seen as near apostasy to do so. The more the adherents of Christianity and Islam are socialized into viewing their respective traditions as apolitical faith traditions, the fainter the prophetic voice becomes.

It is not just the way Christianity and Islam become constructed as depoliticized religious traditions that leads to the loss of the prophetic, however. The focus on individual piety caused in large part by the advance of secularism also leads Christians and Muslims to become afflicted with what we might term Religious-Identity Obsession Syndrome. Christianity and Islam devolve into religious-identity labels to be worn like name tags. They cease to be traditions that lead to deep spiritual reflection and transformation. The reasons for this loss of spiritual depth are complex, and I cannot discuss them in detail here (though I will go into some depth on this topic in chapter five). I dealt with this dynamic extensively in my 2012 book *Radically Open: Transcending Religious Identity in an Age of Anxiety*. But I should point out here how the superficiality of Christian religious identity obsession came home to me in a big way through a recent experience.

Because of the provocative title of my 2009 book *Was Jesus a Muslim?* I fully expected to hear howls of protest from conservative Christians soon after the book's publication. Yet the silence was deafening for more than three years. This all changed dramatically, however, in July 2012 when the conservative website CampusReform.org published an article alerting their readers to an Iowa college professor who had published a book arguing that Jesus was a Muslim. This article quickly went viral and was reposted all over the conservative blogosphere, appearing in such high-profile sources as *World Net Daily* and *Fox Nation*. It also appeared on Bill O'Reilly's *Daily Blog*, and even on Islamophobia queen Pamela Geller's *Atlas Shrugs*. Soon, my e-mail inbox was flooded with all kinds of hateful e-mail containing vile Islamophobic rants. Officials at Luther College received calls for my firing. How—these callers wanted to know—could Luther College employ a professor who lacked even a rudimentary knowledge of historical chronology? Everyone knows that Jesus lived six hundred years before Muhammad. It is chronologically impossible for him to have been a Muslim.

Not surprisingly, not a single one of the "news reporters" who perpetuated this story had even bothered to read my book. On the very first page I make clear that I am not denying the historical reality of Jesus's Jewish identity. I know the chronology! The question I raise—Was Jesus a Muslim?—is far more nuanced than the simple chronological claim that my critics were assuming. But conservative Christians have become so caught up today in a superficial religious-identity obsession that the mere suggestion that religious identities may be more nebulous than we think is just too much for many to handle. My critics could not even take the time to read my book and engage its argument before flying off into apoplectic fits at this perceived affront to their hard-and-fast religious-identity claims: Jesus is owned by Christians. Period! He cannot be a Muslim in any sense of the word, and anyone who would dare suggest otherwise must be the devil incarnate (or brain-dead, as one website claimed I must be). Still today, a review of my book remains on Amazon.com by a reviewer who gives the book one star, who eviscerates it in his comments, but who confesses all along that he has not read a single word of it! When Christians and

Muslims become so caught up in superficial claims to religious identity that they spend their time vehemently policing the mutually exclusive boundaries they create between their carefully constructed religious traditions, the prophetic voice suffers a rather ignominious death.

There is no mystery about why the prophetic heart of Christianity and Islam has so starkly receded in recent times. The individualistic, pietistic, depoliticized turn taken by Christianity and Islam in the contemporary secular world removes all motivation to engage a prophetic voice. Recovery of this voice will require a jihad. But what exactly is a jihad? Must we all become Islamic terrorists? Absolutely not, as the next chapter will make abundantly clear.

3

Waging a Jihad for Jihad

The best jihad is to speak the truth before a tyrant ruler.
—TRADITIONAL SAYING OF THE PROPHET MUHAMMAD

Tarek Mehanna's audacious linking of jihad with the American
Revolution will outrage many Americans, not least because the pervasive Islamophobic environment of contemporary America has distorted the
fundamental Islamic concept of jihad completely beyond recognition. We really do believe that jihad is by definition a specifically anti-American declara-
tion of Islamic holy war. How can the American Revolution be understood as
a jihad when jihad itself is an anti-American idea? Events like the 9/11 attacks
have certainly not helped. What more evidence could we want of the Muslim
crusade against America than the image of hijacked airliners crashing into
the World Trade Center and the Pentagon with such catastrophic results?
Islam must be a religion of anti-American violence and jihad its preferred
method, right? Perhaps not. There is much more to this story.

First, let me acknowledge what I am sure many of my critics will glad-
ly point out: it would be utterly foolish to deny the existence of Muslims
who engage in gratuitously violent actions in order to advance an (often
anti-American) political agenda—the Taliban in Afghanistan; al-Qaeda in
Afghanistan, Iraq, Yemen, and other places; al-Shabab in Somalia; Hamas

and Hizbollah in Palestine; and of course ISIS in Iraq and Syria. Violent Muslims indeed exist. But is the mere existence of Muslim groups that resort to violence proof of an inherently violent Islam that is bent on conquering the world through jihad? Before answering this question, we might first pause to consider the following.

Some of the most flagrant displays of violence unleashed in the world over the last thirty years have been carried out not by Muslim terrorists but by the United States military. (If we go back a few more decades, we find the United States as the only country ever to deploy nuclear weapons against another sovereign nation.) Al-Qaeda may have killed nearly three thousand Americans on 9/11, but America's response (the wars in Afghanistan and Iraq) led to the deaths of more than ten thousand Muslims and the utter devastation of entire countries. In December of 2012 the United States was shocked and horrified by the slaughter of twenty elementary-school children by a deranged gunman in Newtown, Connecticut. Yet, innocent children have been killed by U.S. drone strikes in Pakistan and Yemen without so much as a whimper of American protest. Muslims have certainly not cornered the market on violence. The American military through its shock-and-awe campaigns has established itself as the premier purveyor of extraordinary violence employed for strategic political interests operating in the world today. Does this mean that America as a nation is bent on the destruction of Islam and the domination of the world? Well, I know of no official policy that says so. (President George W. Bush was fond of pointing out that we were not at war with Islam.) Why then do we so easily jump to the conclusion that the existence of violent Muslims is evidence of an inherently violent Muslim crusade against America when the undeniable existence of American violence is not considered evidence of an American crusade against Islam? We jump to this unwarranted conclusion simply under the influence of Islamophobic discourse. Anything having to do with Islam is automatically under suspicion in contemporary Western culture.

The stereotypical image of a violent Islam bent on world domination results from a well-funded campaign of Islamophobia perpetuated by high-profile Islamophobic figures like Robert Spencer, Pamela Geller, Daniel Pipes, and others. These Islamophobic stereotypes are perpetuated in the media in part to justify heavy-handed military ventures in Muslim lands. Citizens are much more likely to support military invasions of the Muslim world if they believe that we are fighting an enemy that poses an existential threat to our values and our very way of life. But, tragically, none of this is true. Sure, there are small groups of Muslims scattered around the world who harbor dreams of world domination and look to violence as a way to bring it about. But their numbers are minuscule and their power severely limited. They pose no more existential threat to America than an injured gazelle poses to a lion on the Serengeti Plain. The vast majority of the world's one and a half billion Muslims harbor no such crusader ambitions and are no more violent than a group of Quakers at a candlelight vigil. So what is jihad if it is not an anti-American campaign of holy war?

To answer this question, we might be tempted to consult one of the many books on jihad currently available on the commercial book market. But this would be a huge mistake. The Islamophobic environment in America is so deeply rooted, and the identification of jihad with holy war so thoroughly entrenched in the American psyche that virtually all the books published on jihad for the general reading public only serve to perpetuate the kinds of stereotypes I am trying to dispel. For example, Gilles Kepel's *Jihad: The Trail of Political Islam* fails to consider any interpretation of jihad besides those perpetuated by contemporary Islamic extremists. Surely these extremists do view their work as jihad, but the title of Kepel's book gives the false impression that this is the only understanding of jihad current among Muslims. Likewise, Reuven Firestone's *Jihad: The Origin of Holy War* clearly buys into the facile jihad-equals-holy-war misrepresentation. At least Kepel and Firestone are reputable scholars, the narrowness of their approach to jihad notwithstanding. Such is not the case with many other jihad books that appear to have been written for no other purpose than to fan the flames of Islamophobia.

Andrew Bostom's *The Legacy of Jihad: Islamic Holy War and the Fate of Non-Muslims* is a 759-page tome purporting to provide documentary evidence of Islam's inherently violent ways through its wretched treatment of religious minorities over the span of a millennium. The problem here is that Bostom is not an Islamic historian (he is a medical doctor); the book bears a foreword by Ibn Warraq, a noted anti-Muslim polemicist; and the book is published by Prometheus Books, a secular-humanist publisher with a strong antireligion bias. Paul Fregosi's *Jihad in the West: Muslim Conquests from the 7th to the 21st Centuries* is another entry into the Islam-is-inherently-violent sweepstakes (also published by Prometheus). And we can't fail to take notice of best-selling apocalyptic author Hal Lindsey's *The Everlasting Hatred: The Roots of Jihad*. The title says it all!

The memoir genre is not much better. Omar Nasiri's *Inside the Jihad: My Life with Al-Qaeda* perpetuates the jihad-equals-terrorism stereotype from the perspective of a former al-Qaeda member. Walid Shoebat's *Why I Left Jihad: The Root of Terrorism and the Return of Radical Islam* does much the same, while Jerry Rassamni's *From Jihad to Jesus: An Ex-Militant's Journey of Faith* recounts the "conversion" of a radical Muslim to evangelical Christianity. (This title should not be confused with the title of the book you are currently reading!) More popular, perhaps, are J. M. Berger's *Jihad Joe: Americans Who Go to War in the Name of Islam* and Igor Baranko's *Jihad*, a futuristic novel about a Russian dictator (à la Vladimir Putin?) in the year 2040 who has a vision to invoke the spirit of Genghis Khan to create an empire reaching from the Pacific Ocean to the Atlantic. Jihad as a strategy of global conquest has deeply captured the American imagination and animated its deepest fears. As a result, the commercial book market is the last place to go looking for reasoned, substantive, and accurate approaches to jihad. I will try to correct the record by considering what Islamic sources actually say about jihad.

First and perhaps most important is to recognize that *jihad* simply does not mean "holy war." Jihad is not an attempt to use force to convert others to Islam. *Jihad* at its most basic level simply means "struggle." To engage in jihad is literally to expend effort trying to accomplish something difficult to achieve. In a specifically Islamic context, it means to struggle in the way of God. But exactly what this means is not explicitly stated in the Qur'an. So Muslim scholars are left to infer a variety of interpretations. One common interpretation makes a distinction between two different types of jihad: a greater jihad and a lesser jihad. The greater jihad is the personal spiritual struggle against one's own soul to live in accordance with the will of God. The lesser jihad is the struggle to transform the political, economic, and social structures of society in accordance with what are believed to be divinely revealed imperatives. But not all thinkers accept the existence of a greater jihad. (This interpretation is more common among those Muslims who have been influenced by Sufi mysticism, which emphasizes the internal spiritual struggle.)

Some view jihad simply as a type of defensive warfare. In this view, Islam is not an inherently violent religion. But Muslims have the right to defend themselves against aggression, and when this aggression comes in the form of violent warfare, Muslims have the right to wage a violent jihad in defense of the homeland. Still other thinkers see jihad as an offensive struggle. According to this view, its purpose is to bring the structures of society (political, economic, social) into alignment with God's will, but because secular society generally resists such a transformation, a jihad (a struggle) is necessary to bring this transformation about. Still other thinkers view jihad as a nonviolent struggle to bring about a just peace in the world.

The Islamic tradition is large and complex, and it should surprise no one that a term like *jihad* has such a multivalent history. But despite the different interpretations of the term and concept, little evidence exists that jihad has ever been understood as the struggle for world domination by any more than at most a very small handful of Muslims, who, fortunately, lack the ability to even attempt to bring such a plan to fulfillment. To get a better sense of how early Muslims understood jihad, we will take a closer look at what this idea means in the Qur'an. This will be followed by a discussion of the meaning of jihad in the work of two interesting contemporary thinkers, and then by a portrait of jihad in action in the life of Emir Abd el-Kader, the famous nineteenth-century Algerian freedom fighter. The following analysis will throw into stark relief the utter failure of jihad in contemporary Islam and will lead to reflections on how the recovery of an authentic jihad might help to reignite a Muslim prophetic voice. Jihad is not the scary idea the Islamophobes would have us believe it is. We cannot allow ourselves to be duped into the perpetuation of harmful stereotypes, but ironically must begin to wage a jihad for jihad!

JIHAD IN THE QUR'AN AND EARLY ISLAM

Given the attention garnered by the term *jihad* in the modern media, it may be surprising to learn that noun *jihad* occurs a mere four times in the Qur'an (Surahs 9:24; 22:78; 25:52; 60:1). The verbal form *jahada* is more common—though with only twenty-eight occurrences, the concept of waging a jihad is not nearly as common in the Qur'an as one might expect. Moreover, the Qur'an makes explicit distinctions between the term *jahada* ("struggle") and concepts like war (*harb*) and killing (*qatala*). So, contrary to popular belief, the Qur'an makes no essential connection between jihad and violence.

To be sure, it is not clear exactly what the Qur'an *does* envision when employing the verb *jahada*, but we will need to cast a wide semantic net since in two cases, *jahada* actually describes the actions not of Muslims but of those who might try to lead Muslims astray. Surah 29:8 has, for example,

> We have enjoined on man kindness to parents: but if they strive (*jahada*) to force you to join with me anything of which you have no knowledge, obey them not.[1]

The almost-identical admonition is repeated in Surah 31:15. The point here is that parents should be highly esteemed by their children. However, if parents attempt to lead their children away from the Islamic message of the absolute oneness of God, children should then refuse to obey the will of their parents. Since the term *jahada* can be employed to characterize the striving of the parents to force their children to *abandon* the Islamic message, jihad in the Qur'an is clearly not a universal call to convert the whole world to Islam! Jihad is not holy war.

Outside of these two noteworthy exceptions, the Qur'an does employ *jahada* consistently to describe the actions of the followers of the Islamic message. But exactly what actions are being prescribed? Consider the following three texts:

> Surely those who believe and those who emigrate and struggle (*jahada*) in the way of God may hope for His benevolence. (2:218)

> O you who believe, follow God, seek His path, and struggle (*jahada*) in His way; you may have success. (5:35)

> Those who believe and emigrate and struggle (*jahada*) in the way of God with their wealth and their soul have a greater reward in the sight of God. (9:20)

To these verses could be added many more featuring similar formulaic language. Struggling in the way of God is equated with believing, emigrating, and following in God's path as the kinds of behaviors necessary for the followers of the Islamic message. "Emigrating" in these passages makes reference to the *hijra*, the movement of Muhammad and his small group of followers from Mecca to Medina in 622 CE in order to avoid persecution in Mecca: the *hijra* is a seminal event that marks the first year of the Muslim calendar. Not all of Muhammad's followers were keen on making this journey into a new life in a new city, however. So the Qur'an singles out those

---

1. English translations of the Qur'an tend to provide many different English renderings of *jahada/jihad*. I have thus provided my own translations to make it easier to see the context in which the Arabic word *jahada* is being used. These translations are adopted from Asad, *The Message of the Qur'an*.

who emigrated to Medina for special praise. When we consider the importance of the *hijra* for Muslim identity along with the fundamental nature of belief, the idea that the Qur'an repeatedly places "struggling in the way of God" alongside the actions of believing and *hijra* implies that struggling (jihad) is considered one of the fundamental actions defining what it means to be a Muslim. Jihad is not some optional activity that Muslims can engage in if they so desire. Engaging in jihad is fundamental to Muslim identity.

But what exactly does it mean to "struggle in the way of God"? The Qur'an is frustratingly ambiguous on this point, leaving the reader to infer what specific actions "struggling in the way of God" might entail. Clarifying this will require a brief detour into the origins of the Islamic movement. Once we have a sense of what Muhammad was trying to accomplish in seventh-century Arabia, we will be in a better position to infer what the Qur'an means by the admonition to "struggle in the way of God."

Unfortunately, this is no easy task. The nature of the nascent Islamic movement is much debated by scholars. Muslims tell a traditional story about the historical development of the Islamic movement, but its historical accuracy is open to question. Some Western scholars have seriously questioned the historical reliability of traditional Muslim sources, claiming that they were written at least 150 years after the events they purport to describe. Such scholars therefore consider the traditional Muslim story to be a hagiographical account influenced more by what was happening in the ninth century when the source documents were written than by the actual historical realities of the seventh century in which Muhammad lived. Consider for comparison that the New Testament Gospels are thought to have been written some forty to sixty years after Jesus's life and are widely considered of dubious historical value. How, then, can we trust documents written 150 years later? This is an important question for which there is no easy answer. But an influential historian of early Islam, Fred M. Donner, has recently developed a middle-ground approach between uncritically taking the Muslim sources at face value and entirely dismissing them altogether as late hagiography, and I think Donner's approach has much to recommend it. A part of his historical reconstruction will therefore be offered here to help answer the question about what "struggling" means in the Qur'an. A more detailed engagement with Donner's reconstruction will be deferred until chapter 4 where it will make more sense in the context of the theme of that chapter. So what do we know about the origins of Islam?

From what we can tell, Islam emerged in the context of a seventh-century Arab society characterized by high levels of violence and social and economic injustice. As I mentioned in the previous chapter, Islam emerged into a society shaped by a tribal honor/shame ethic. One's identity was derived primarily from one's tribal and clan loyalties, and the principle purpose of life was to maintain the honor of one's tribe and clan. If your tribe was dishonored, it was incumbent upon you to work to restore the lost honor. This was usually done by exacting some form of revenge, a method of restoring honor that often led to blood feuds and spirals of violence. In addition to relying on tribal ethics, pre-Islamic Arab society was also polytheistic. A range of gods and goddesses were worshiped in the form of idols, with each clan possessing its own tribal deity.

Into this society Muhammad was born around 570 CE. He was orphaned young and raised by his uncle Abu Talib. He quickly established himself as a trustworthy and righteous individual; these traits made him quite valuable to this fractured society because they placed Muhammad in the position of being able to mediate tribal disputes since he could gain the trust of both sides. These valued traits also brought him success in the caravan trading business, and it was there that he met his first wife, Khadijah. In addition to his righteousness and trustworthiness, Muhammad is said to have possessed a somewhat mystical streak, which led him to engage in periods of quiet reflection and meditation, frequently in a cave outside of his home in Mecca—the Cave of Hira. As the story goes, it was in the year 610, when Muhammad was about forty years old, that the angel Gabriel appeared to him in the Cave of Hira with a revelation from God for the people of Mecca, and ostensibly, the world. This was the first of a series of revelations Muhammad would receive over the next twenty-three years— revelations that would be collected and published in the form of the Qur'an. What was the thrust of the message Muhammad was enjoined to preach to his people?

In the midst of a polytheistic society, Muhammad exhorted his people to abandon their idols and submit themselves in worship to a single overarching deity. Pre-Islamic Arabs already believed in the existence of an all-powerful creator deity known as Al-Lah (which is simply the Arabic phrase "the God"), but they did not believe this supreme deity was interested in or involved in human affairs. Thus, they turned to the lesser deities and worshiped them in the form of idols. For Muhammad, this supreme deity, Allah, was the only god that existed and therefore the only one worthy of worship and submission—hence, his exhortation to abandon idolatry. Let's be clear here. This was not just a theological message.

The Umayyad clan of the Quraysh tribe (Muhammad was from the Quraysh tribe but from a different clan) took responsibility for the worship activities that occurred at a central shrine in Mecca known as the Ka'ba. The Umayyads made a handsome living manufacturing the idols that pilgrims to the Ka'ba would purchase for their worship activities. Thus, Muhammad's call to destroy the idols had a negative economic impact on the Umayyads, to which they did not take kindly. Moreover, Muhammad's call to submit to a single supreme deity rather than to lesser idols representing individual clans and tribes had the effect of overriding the tribal honor/shame ethic. The primary purpose of life was now to live in submission to this one God, not to maintain tribal honor. The oneness of God implied the oneness of humanity living in submission to this one God. The message that Muhammad received was meant to bring about a complete transformation of Arab society: to replace injustice with justice, and violence with peace. In light of the Islamic message, blood feuds were to become a thing of the past under the influence of Islam; the Qur'an is filled with exhortations to care for the poor and to protect widows and orphans.

The Islamic message is beautiful in its simplicity, but as is usually the case with these kinds of grand utopian visions, the devil is always in the details. People who enjoy power and privilege are not quick to give them up. Whole lives were thoroughly invested in the idolatrous tribal honor/shame system—or, that is, the people who derived benefit from the system were invested in it! Predictably, then, they rejected Muhammad's message, and when Muhammad's uncle died, leaving him without tribal protection, the way was clear for Muhammad's adversaries to plan his assassination. But as luck would have it, Muhammad was invited in 622 CE to migrate to the desert oasis town of Yathrib, some two hundred miles north of Mecca, to mediate a tribal dispute. This removed him from the threats to his life in Mecca and became a fertile ground for the Islamic message. In Yathrib (which came to be known as Medina) Muhammad became the leader of a growing movement dedicated to developing his vision of justice and peace, and to rendering it a historical reality. But his Meccan adversaries did not go quietly, and it became necessary for Muhammad and his growing band of Muslims to engage in military battles with the Meccans to preserve the expanding Islamic movement.

What does any of this have to do with jihad? Recall from the discussion above that the Qur'an regularly lists struggling in the way of God along with believing and emigrating (to Medina) as actions incumbent on anyone who would consider himself or herself a part of the Islamic movement. The attempt to bring about a divinely ordained system that would lead to greater levels of justice and peace provoked resistance from those who benefited from the unjust status quo. So the Muslims had to struggle in order to render this vision a historical reality. This, I believe, is jihad: the necessity and willingness to struggle against the obstacles preventing social transformation toward greater levels of justice and peace. Those that benefit from the unjust status quo will always resist change. Change, therefore, will always entail a struggle, and this is what it means in the Qur'an to engage in jihad, to "struggle in the way of God."

It is clear in the Qur'an that becoming a Muslim requires more than merely believing in the Islamic message in one's individual heart. Islam cannot be mere passive intellectual assent to a set of doctrines or theological propositions. Islam cannot be made to sit easily with the unjust status quo and be defined as an apolitical set of theological propositions. Surah 4:95 reads as follows:

> Not equal are those believers who sit at home and receive no hurt and those who struggle in the way of God with their wealth and their souls. God has granted a higher grade to those who struggle with their wealth and their souls than to those who sit at home. Unto all God has promised good, but those who struggle he has distinguished above those who sit at home with a special reward.

To be Muslim must cost something. One must be engaged in the struggle for social transformation, bearing the risks that attend such behavior. (Just ask Martin Luther King Jr. and other civil rights leaders if the struggle for social change is risky!) Islam cannot be just a movement of individual piety (as it has become for far too many Muslims today). Jihad is an essential characteristic of Islam.

This more political understanding of Islam is beautifully illustrated in the biographical account of Muhammad penned in the eighth century by Ibn Ishaq (but only extant in a ninth-century recension). Ibn Ishaq tells the story of how Muhammad, because of the persecution faced by his early followers at the hands of his Meccan adversaries, arranged to have some of his followers temporarily sent to the Christian kingdom of Abyssinia for protection. Once the Muslims were safely in Abyssinia and out of the reach of Meccan persecution, some Meccan leaders traveled to Abyssinia, imploring the Abyssinian leaders to return their Muslim guests to Arabia. The Meccan leaders accused the Muslims of following a false belief that the Abyssinians wouldn't want their Christian people exposed to. The Abyssinian king refused this request until he had the chance to talk to the Muslims themselves and learn about their beliefs.

Calling the Muslims before him, the Abyssinian king inquired about the charges leveled at them by the Meccans. One of the Muslims, Ja'far ibn Abu Talib, responded:

> O king, we were an uncivilized people, worshipping idols, eating corpses, committing abominations, breaking natural ties, treating guests badly, and our strong devoured our weak. Thus we were until God sent us an apostle whose lineage, truth, trustworthiness, and clemency we know. He summoned us to acknowledge God's unity and to worship him and to renounce the stones and images which we and our father's formerly worshipped. He commanded us to speak the truth, be faithful to our engagements, mindful of ties of kinship and kindly hospitality, and to refrain from crimes and bloodshed. He forbade us to commit abominations and to speak lies, and to devour the property of orphans, to vilify chaste women.[2]

Upon hearing Ja'far's speech, the king immediately recognized the connection between the message of Islam and the message of Jesus and pledged his firm support for the Muslims, granting them protection in Abyssinia for as long as needed.

Important here is the way Ja'far characterizes the Islamic message in relation to the character of pre-Islamic Arabia. He describes the Muslims as formerly being uncivilized idol worshipers who committed abominations and lived in a society where "the strong devoured the weak." But since the advent of Islam they no longer commit such abominations, nor do they devour the property of orphans. Please note that the strong can only devour the weak in a society *institutionally* set up to allow for this type of economic exploitation. Exploitation of the poor is not an individualistic activity. It occurs only where political, economic, and social structures are intentionally designed to concentrate wealth in the hands of the few at the expense of the many. So Ja'far is strongly indicating that one of the aims of the Islamic message was to eliminate institutionalized economic injustice in society.

2. Guillaume, *Life of Muhammad*, 151.

And it stands to reason that any attempt to fundamentally transform economic structures in this way will require a jihad today—a struggle.

A jihad for justice can take many forms. There are all kinds of ways to work for the transformation of society. Force and violence are certainly one way, but they are far from the only way, and may not even be the most effective way (more on this below). And given that the Qur'an always makes a clear distinction between jihad, war, and killing, it would seem that the qur'anic notion of jihad encompasses any behavior that has as its goal social transformation, regardless of the particular method. Given modern stereotypes about jihad and about Islam as an inherently violent movement bent on world domination, it is important to take a minute here to address the issue of violence in the Qur'an and the early Islamic movement. Muhammad manifestly was involved in military activity when necessary to protect his nascent movement from the desires of its opponents to wipe it out. But is it the case that the early Muslims were bloodthirsty tyrants?

Many who think so point to Surah 9 as scriptural proof of early Islam's warrior tendencies and jihad as its violent method. Many verses of this Surah are frequently cited as evidence that Muhammad exhorted the early Muslims to fight against and kill those who did not accept the Islamic message. The truth, however, is far more complex. Let's consider a few of these supposed violent verses.

Surah 9:5 reads:

> But when the forbidden months are past, then fight and slay the polytheists wherever you find them. Seize them and beleaguer them, and lie in wait for them in every stratagem of war . . .

The Arabic word rendered "polytheists" here is *mushrikin*, which means those who practice *shirk*, the act of associating other people or things with God: this is the supreme apostasy in Islam. The surah clearly refers to the polytheistic members of the Quraysh tribe who resisted the Islamic message of monotheism and who tried to violently destroy the Islamic movement. Faced with this existential threat, the Muslims are exhorted here to take action against this threat; the use of military tactics is permitted in self-defense. Interestingly, the word *jihad* is not used here. Still, many would point to this verse as evidence for early Islam's warmongering ways. But such an interpretation is only tenable if one ignores the second half of the verse (which opponents of Islam typically do). Surah 9:5 continues:

. . . but if they repent and establish regular prayers and practice regular charity, then open the way for them; for God is oft-forgiving, most merciful.

Yes, the Qur'an permits Muslims to use warfare to defend themselves in the face of attack, but it also makes clear that the enemies of Islam must be given every chance to repent, and if they do they must be forgiven and treated with mercy.

This emphasis on mercy is captured in a brief story told about a young man named Usamah, who killed an enemy combatant during battle despite the adversary's having uttered the Shahadah—the Muslim confession of faith—at the point of Usamah's sword. Please note that sincerely confessing the Shahadah is said to render one a Muslim, and violence should never be used against a fellow Muslim. So Usamah's actions seem to go against basic Islamic norms. He, therefore, tried to justify his killing of the man to Muhammad with the argument that the man's profession of faith was insincere and was meant only to preserve his life. In response, Muhammad castigated Usamah with the words, "And so thou didst split open his heart to know if he spake the truth or if he lied!"[3] At this, Usamah pledged to never again slay anyone who uttered the Shahadah. Force can be used only against clear enemies, and mercy should always trump the desire to kill.

Verse 6 of Surah 9 then continues this theme:

> If one among the polytheists asks you for asylum, grant it to him so that he may hear the Word of God; then escort him to where he can be secure. That is because they are men without knowledge.

Once again, enemies must be treated with mercy if they lay down their arms. There is simply no sense in which the Qur'an exhorts its readers to engage in gratuitous violence or to try to force people to convert to Islam. The qur'anic dictate is to peacefully try to persuade people to accept the Islamic message (Surah 2:256 famously says, "There is no compulsion in religion") and to treat those who resist with mercy and justice so long as they do not wage war against the Islamic movement. Only if they do so is it then allowable to engage in war as a method of defense. The qur'anic worldview is no more inherently violent than U.S. foreign policy!

Please note that none of the verses in Surah 9 that explicitly call for the use of military activity ever employ the word *jihad* to denote this activity (the root *qatala* is normally employed to denote warfare). The root *jahada*

---

3. Quoted in Lings, *Muhammad*, 275.

does appear ten times in the Surah, but only twice are there any hints that it might refer to war. For example, see verse 41:

> Go forth, whether lightly or heavily, and struggle (*jahada*) with your wealth and your souls in the way of God. That is best for you if only you knew.

Going forth "lightly" or "heavily" may refer to going out to the battlefield armed either lightly or heavily. Whatever weapons you have must be brought out to the "struggle." In this cryptic verse, jihad might be referring to war. So also in verse 81:

> Those who were left behind rejoiced in their inaction behind the back of the Apostle of God: they hated to struggle (*jahada*) with their wealth and their souls in the way of God. They said, "Go not forth in the heat." Say, "The fire of Hell is worse." If only they could understand.

Some members of the Islamic movement may have purposely resisted going out to war during the summer heat. (Remember these battles would have taken place in the Arabian desert where it can reach 120 degrees!) But they are castigated for their sneaky intransigence. Jihad is incumbent on all Muslims when a threat is faced.

So Surah 9 does make provisions for allowable warfare, and it does at least hint that this warfare can be subsumed under the rubric of jihad. But clearly in the Qur'an *jihad* has a much wider semantic range. War may be a form of jihad in specific circumstances, but jihad is much more than war. It is the fundamental aspect of struggling to bring about a social transformation toward justice and peace and can take many forms, nonviolent ones included. There is simply no evidence in the Qur'an for the stereotypical image of an inherently violent Islam bent on forced conversion and world domination. And outside of the Qur'an, there is interesting documentary evidence that seems to reinforce this point. This is where Fred M. Donner's reinterpretation of Islamic origins becomes important.

Donner, an Islamic historian at the University of Chicago, has written *Muhammad and the Believers: At the Origins of Islam*, a book offering a fundamentally new reconstruction of the nature of the early Islamic movement. Donner accepts the general outline of the traditional narrative of Islamic origins but observes that the message of the Qur'an seems to be addressed to people referred to as "believers" rather than to Muslims. (The phrase "O you who believe" occurs more than a thousand times in the

Qur'an; "Muslim" only forty-two times.) Donner reasons that the members of the earliest movement spawned by the qur'anic revelations must have referred to themselves as believers, and he therefore brands early Islam a Believers' movement. Moreover, there is evidence that this Believers' movement was what Donner calls "ecumenical," and likely included Christians, Jews, Zoroastrians, and former pagan Arabs who had turned to the monotheistic message of Islam. The early Islamic movement does not appear to have arisen as a new religious movement—Islam—trying to rival Judaism and Christianity. Rather, Donner dubs it a monotheistic reform movement.

Donner's argument for the "ecumenical" nature of the Believers' movement may appear shocking at first, not least to those Muslims afflicted with Religious-Identity Obsession Syndrome. If there is one thing both Muslims and the opponents of Islam could probably agree on, it is that Islam functions in the modern world as an exclusive religious identity clearly in opposition to Judaism, Christianity, Hinduism, and all other so-called religions (especially as Islam is articulated by apologists like Zakir Naik). We might be tempted to simply ignore Donner's claim as merely the romantic notion of an ivory-tower scholar insulated from the realities of life in the real world. But Donner's view has some compelling archaeological evidence standing behind it that I will spell out in more detail in chapter five. I beg the reader's patience on this. This evidence will make better sense in the context of that later discussion. And my purpose here is to focus on how Donner's work challenges the Islam-is-inherently-violent stereotype. We will take up the "ecumenical" nature of early Islam with Donner's help later.

According to Donner, there is scant evidence for a gratuitously violent Believers' movement. Archaeological excavations have turned up little evidence of warfare, destruction, or other forms of violence in the lands "conquered" by early Muslims (or Believers). According to Donner, it appears that

> the area underwent a gradual process of social and cultural transformation that did not involve a violent and sudden destruction of urban or rural life at all. In town after town, we find evidence of churches that are not destroyed—but, rather, continue in use for a century or more after the "conquest"—or evidence that new churches (with dated mosaic floors) were being constructed.[4]

4. Donner, *Muhammad and the Believers*, 107.

If Islam was a confessional movement demanding the conversion of "conquered" peoples at the point of a sword, the adherents of Christianity and other religions, according to Donner, would almost certainly have resisted, and this resistance would surely have left its marks on the literature of the period. "But no significant Christian or other polemics against the Believers' doctrines appear for almost a century."[5]

This evidence is hard to square with the stereotypical image of a fundamentally new religious movement waging violent jihad against other religious groups on their way to world domination. But if Donner is right about early Islam being an ecumenical "Believers'" movement whose goal was to bring about the transformation of an unjust and violent society, the evidence begins to make more sense. In Donner's view,

> The predominantly West Arabian leaders of the Believers' movement were not asking the people of Syria-Palestine, Egypt, and Iraq to give up their ancestral religion to embrace another—that surely would have led to violent confrontation. But they were imposing their political hegemony on the conquered populations, requiring them to pay taxes, and asking them, at least initially, to affirm their belief in one God and in the Last Day, and to affirm their commitment to living righteously and to avoid sin. They were, in short, establishing a new political order and perhaps advancing a program of monotheistic (and moral?) reform but not proposing religious revolution or demanding conversion to a new faith.[6]

The evidence is compelling for a view of Islamic origins that differs in detail from the traditional view but retains the core message. Muhammad was a prophetic figure in seventh-century Arabia leading a movement whose goal was not the establishing of a new religion but the transformation of a violent and unjust society. Calling all people to unite in submission to a single overarching deity was a powerful attempt to heal the tribal fracturing of society that authorized so much bloodshed, an attempt to tame the human ego and its unquenchable thirst for exploitative power. Jihad was the method for realizing this prophetic transformation—a kind of jihad we are sorely in need of today as our ego-driven lives of unending material consumption run roughshod over any attempt to realize a world of justice, peace, and environmental sustainability.

5. Ibid., 109.
6. Ibid.

Recall from the previous chapter the idea that religion thought of as a separate category of experience clearly distinct from politics and economics is a modern, Western (and largely Christian) idea. There was no such concept as religion at the time of Muhammad. Islam is based on the unity and integrity of all experience such that no meaningful distinction between religion and politics is even conceivable. The affirmation of the existence of a single deity to whom all people owe their willing submission carries direct implications for the whole of society, political and economic life included. Jihad, then, must be understood as a political force—a force for the transformation of society, not just the transformation of an individual's heart. But the religionization of Islam in the contemporary world along with the Islamophobic caricature of jihad as holy war has served to diminish the role for jihad as Islam has been domesticated and transformed into a personal spiritual tradition that easily accommodates to systems of injustice. The loss of jihad is truly the loss of the prophetic. Fortunately, modern examples exist of Muslims who provide important reflections on the nature of jihad or who demonstrate jihad at its best in action. Muslims desperately need to reengage these figures. I will set the stage by engaging them here.

JIHAD IN CONTEMPORARY ISLAM

The historical journey of jihad in Muslim thought is long and complex and therefore impossible to do justice to here; this history has been admirably chronicled by Richard Bonney's *Jihad: From Qur'an to Bin Laden*. I do, however, want to consider the works of two contemporary Muslim thinkers who have offered interpretations of jihad particularly useful for any attempt to reclaim the prophetic heart of the Islamic tradition: Sayyid Qutb and Ahmed Afzaal. Further, I want to highlight one extraordinary historical figure who is, or at least should be, a model for jihad in action: Emir Abd el-Kader.

Sayyid Qutb

Who is Sayyid Qutb? While you may not know the name, it is a name with the power to ring alarm bells within the national-security apparatus of the United States, a surprising fact given that Qutb died in 1966. Why do we fear a Muslim who has not walked the planet for nearly a half century? Are there not enough living Muslims to fear that we have to conjure up threats from long-dead ones too? What is it about a dead scholar that provokes so much fear and loathing in the West today?

Sayyid Qutb was one of the most influential Islamic teachers in the Arab world in the middle of the twentieth century and became a leading spokesperson for the Muslim Brotherhood in Egypt. Given that the Muslim Brotherhood has been widely considered a terrorist organization (even though it became the duly elected government of Egypt for a year following the Arab Spring), many scholars have pointed a finger at Qutb's work, finding in it a blueprint for Islamic terrorism, including for the work of al-Qaeda. It is without question that Osama bin Laden read the works of Qutb (virtually everyone in the Arab world has), but it is unfair to draw a direct line from Qutb to al-Qaeda. Someone writing in the 1960s cannot possibly be held responsible for how someone else interprets his writing in 2001! After all, I know many Muslims who revere Qutb as one of the great teachers in the Islamic tradition but do not as a result engage in terrorism or other acts of violence. (One such person was even an undergraduate student of mine who is now a PhD candidate in international peacemaking and working for the Carter Center in Atlanta!) So some perspective is in order here. Let's consider Qutb's work outside the Islamophobic framework that distorts his important insights.

Sayyid Qutb was born in 1906 in a small Egyptian village. As an adult he became a secular literary critic and took a job in the Egyptian Ministry of Education during the rule of Gamal Abdel Nasser, the Arab nationalist dictator who ruled Egypt in the 1950s and 1960s. While Qutb's earlier life did not revolve heavily around Islam, this later changed, and Qutb became convinced that Islam held within it the answers for the ills and injustices of Egyptian society. The transformation in his outlook seems to have been aided by a two-year sojourn in the United States (1948–1950), an experience that convinced him of the inability of Western political, economic, and social policies to effect positive change in Egypt. He thus became an outspoken critic of Nasser's rule, charging the dictator with looking to the West for resources to cure Egypt's ills rather than turning toward their own indigenous tradition of Islam. Eventually Qutb quit the Ministry of Education and became active in the Muslim Brotherhood. This activity led to a series of arrests and imprisonments by Nasser, who came to see Qutb as a threat to the stability of his regime. Finally, Qutb was charged (almost certainly falsely) of plotting Nasser's assassination and was executed by the government in 1966. Qutb wrote voluminously throughout his life, penning a widely read commentary on the Qur'an and a fascinating book, *Social Justice in Islam*. But I want to focus here on his most revolutionary work, a small manifesto titled *Milestones*.

Qutb wrote *Milestones* while in prison, and its popularity among the masses led the Egyptian government to quickly ban it, a strategy that backfired by making the book that much more popular. In *Milestones*, Qutb tries to rally an Islamic vanguard to take the initiative in bringing about a social transformation based on Islamic principles. (You can see why Nasser felt threatened!) Such a transformation would, of course, require a jihad to bring it about, and so, not surprisingly, chapter 4 of *Milestones* is titled "Jihad in the Cause of Allah." Many find Qutb's articulation of jihad to be rather aggressive. To be sure, Qutb rejects the notion of jihad as a primarily defensive strategy that can only be legitimately deployed in the face of an attack. Qutb writes:

> Indeed, Islam has the right to take the initiative. Islam is not a heritage of any particular race or country. This is Allah's *din* and it is for the whole world. It has the right to destroy all obstacles in the form of institutions and traditions that restrict man's freedom of choice. It does not attack individuals nor does it force them to accept its beliefs. It attacks institutions and traditions in order to release human beings from their pernicious influence, which distorts human nature and curtails human freedom.[7]

This quotation beautifully sums up Qutb's view of jihad. The purpose of Islam, for him, is the freeing of humans from subordination to other humans so that they are free to submit willingly to God. Qutb wants nothing short of a societal transformation designed to bring about divine submission in all affairs of life, which will lead, he believes, to a more just, peaceful, and humane world. (Remember, he wrote an entire book on social justice in Islam.) But the forces of injustice do not surrender their power willingly, and they frequently use coercive power (and oftentimes violence) to enforce the unjust status quo. Therefore, Qutb believes that Muslims have a duty to use power in return to defeat the institutions and structures that support the unjust status quo.

---

7. Qutb, *Milestones*, 61. The Arabic word *din* here (as also in the Qur'an) is often translated "religion," but since religion is a modern Western concept it can't really mean this. *Din* is better understood as referring to the comprehensive structure for all of life ordained by God, and is best left untranslated since English lacks a single word or phrase that captures the semantic force of *din*.

Qutb's ideas here are not just theoretical. He is not writing *Milestones* from the comfort of the scholar's study. His criticism of Nasser's dictatorial rule landed him in prison where he was tortured. Qutb learned from experience the unquestionable truth that unjust systems are enforced by the exercise of coercive power, and he truly believed that they could only be met by power in return. Qutb is careful to emphasize the freedom of individuals to accept Islam; conversion cannot be forced. People must be persuaded to the Islamic message by preaching and teaching and then given the option to make a decision. He writes:

> Preaching confronts beliefs and ideas while the "movement" tackles material obstacles. Foremost among these is political power resting on a complex of interrelated ideological, racial, class, social, and economic structures. These two approaches—preaching and the movement—in unison confront "the human situation" with all the necessary means to achieve their common goal.[8]

And what is their common goal? For Qutb it is "the achievement of the freedom of man on earth—of all mankind throughout the earth."[9]

Again, Qutb does not consider jihad a purely defensive strategy. Islam is for him a global movement for the freedom of all people to submit willingly to God, a paradigm for life that he believes will issue in a more just, peaceful, and humane world. But if Islam is to take such an initiative, it will certainly meet powerful resistance. If Muslims only preach the Islamic message and hope that hearers willingly respond, they will be sorely disappointed because attitudes are shaped by "a complex of interrelated ideological, racial, class, social, and economic structures" that prevent people from even hearing the Islamic message and even more from being able to accept it. These institutional structures must, therefore, be attacked and dismantled with the same effort that is used to maintain them. This enduring struggle is what constitutes jihad for Qutb.

This is an important insight. Contrary to the stereotype of Qutb as a primitive Muslim extremist fomenting terrorism, his understanding of jihad betrays a rather sophisticated analysis that deserves further comment. Qutb seems to recognize the frequently ignored truth that people's attitudes and beliefs are deeply shaped by the larger institutional structures under whose influence they live. People are not totally free to choose what to think; to believe otherwise is simply the fallacy of our extreme emphasis

8. Ibid., 48.

9. Ibid.

on individualism. In reality, political, economic, and social institutions are powerful shapers of the intellectual mindset of people, restricting their views and limiting the options of what ideas seem rational or socially acceptable. It is clear, for example, that Americans living in the antebellum South did not each individually decide to believe that Africans were sub-human creatures destined to a life of slavery. This idea was powerfully socialized into them by the system of institutionalized slavery itself, a system that permeated all aspects of their lives from their earliest childhood memories. We have all been socialized into particular worldviews far more than we realize. We are not as free to choose what to think as we like to believe.

Given this, Qutb recognizes how fruitless it will be to simply preach the Islamic message, trying to call to a mindset of submission people who have been thoroughly socialized into a system based on human sovereignty and ego fulfillment. Those who are socialized into a secular mindset are not really free to choose an Islamic mindset any more than white Southerners were "free" to choose to believe in the equality of Africans. Thus, Qutb believes it is crucial that people be freed from the influence of secular institutions before they will be able to choose Islam. It is the dismantling of these secular institutions that constitutes jihad for Qutb. Of course, Qutb does want to replace the secular institutions with Islamic ones, placing people back under the influence of a new socializing force. But there is no hypocrisy here. He recognizes rightly that there is no neutral ground. We will live either by submission to God or by a belief in human sovereignty and self-sufficiency. There is really no other alternative. Qutb simply opts for submission to God and believes that Muslims have just as much right to take the initiative to bring this system about as secularists do to enforce secular institutions.

Qutb's call to dismantle the institutions of the secular system will open him to the charge of advocating a form of violent jihad. But let's turn the spotlight back once again on U. S. foreign policy. How did America respond when Iraqi dictator Saddam Hussein invaded Kuwait in 1991, threatening the West's oil supply? Did we rely on diplomacy and harsh words? Of course not! Then-president George H. W. Bush assembled an international coalition to meet violence with violence by militarily pushing Hussein out of Kuwait in Operation Desert Storm. How did America respond to the injustice of the 9/11 attacks? By negotiating with our enemies? No! By launching a military invasion of two sovereign nations inordinately killing far more innocent civilians than died in the 9/11 attack itself. Qutb's understanding of jihad as constituting reciprocal force is no less inherently violent than any operation the U.S. government has engaged in during recent decades. Violence is a tricky thing.

Recall how the 2013 death of a beloved Nobel Peace Prize laureate unleashed a worldwide torrent of affection for a paragon of peace and reconciliation, despite the fact that he once wrote:

> But if sabotage did not produce the results we wanted, we were prepared to move on to the next stage: guerilla warfare and terrorism.[10]

These, of course, are the words of Nelson Mandela. They recount his experience as leader of the underground militant wing of the African National Congress during the struggle against apartheid. Mandela not only trained as a militant, but he actually helped carry out several violent attacks—something there is no evidence that Sayyid Qutb ever did. So Qutb's reputation as the paradigm example of the violent Muslim extremist is really just an Islamophobic reflex that obscures the work of a far more sophisticated thinker.

Nevertheless, not all will agree that Qutb's very traditional formulation of Islam constitutes a global force for justice and peace, and there is certainly room to criticize Qutb on issues of women's rights and authentic tolerance for those who freely decide not to adopt the Islamic message once they have been freed to do so. But Qutb's rejection of a religionized Islam defined as an individualistic faith tradition and his interpretation of jihad within a more politicized understanding of Islam is an important insight. The unjust status quo that socializes people into mindsets that perpetuate injustice is enforced by power and must be met by power in return. A prophetic Islam (what other kind of Islam is there?) will be inconsistent, then, with a religionized Islam that eschews political activity. Still, Qutb's call for a jihad that attacks social structures may still leave him open to the charge of advocating violence, but our next thinker will brilliantly address this issue.

Ahmed Afzaal

Ahmed Afzaal differs from Sayyid Qutb in many ways. Qutb spent most of his life in Egypt (except for his brief stint in the United States). Afzaal, a

---

10. Mandela, *Long Walk to Freedom*, 246.

native of Pakistan, now lives and works in the United States as a professor of religious studies at a Lutheran college. Sayyid Qutb I never met, but Ahmed Afzaal I consider a colleague and friend. But despite the differences, Afzaal shares with Qutb a belief in the fundamental importance of jihad to Muslim identity, but with a twist. For Afzaal, the only effective form jihad can take in the contemporary world is a nonviolent one.

In a small booklet titled *Jihad without Violence,* Afzaal lays out a compelling case for why nonviolent resistance to injustice is the only method of resistance with any chance of success in the contemporary world. First, he observes that "effort is required to resist and overcome the forces that pull us away from God, that lead us further from the path of God, be these forces within a person's soul or out there in society."[11] Afzaal here implies the commonly held distinction between the greater jihad (the internal struggle) and the lesser jihad (the external struggle). But he continues with a strong affirmation of the absolutely fundamental nature of jihad for Muslim identity:

> Strictly speaking, then, jihad cannot be conceived as one particular item in the list of all the obligations that human beings owe to their Creator. Instead, jihad is the ever-present struggle that underlies—and allows—the realization of any and all such obligations. This makes jihad an indispensable part of being and becoming a muslim, i.e., a person who willingly submits to God's moral will.[12]

To paraphrase: no jihad, no Islam. And hence a religionized non-prophetic Islam ceases to be Islam.

For Afzaal as for Qutb, to work for the transformation of social structures in line with the moral imperatives of the Qur'an is a fundamental obligation placed on all Muslims, but Afzaal believes that "violence is rapidly becoming one of the least effective means for changing social structures and institutions."[13] This is primarily due to the development of the modern nation-state and its ability to co-opt power and violence in support of its own agenda. Modern nation-states have large standing militaries with access to all the latest technologies of war. There is such a wide disparity between the resources available to ordinary citizens and those available to nation-states that it is virtually impossible for a popular movement

11. Afzaal, *Jihad without Violence*, 3.

12. Ibid.

13. Ibid., 19.

to achieve any kind of positive result through armed resistance. (This is why the U.S. gun lobby's position on arming citizens to defend themselves against the excessive power of government is so preposterous.) Al-Qaeda may have killed nearly three thousand Americans in the 9/11 attack, but American power for good or ill still dominates the world. Terrorism rarely achieves its objectives.

But, Afzaal observes, the modern nation-state is increasingly reliant for its own legitimacy on the willing consent and cooperation of its citizens. This is due to advances in literacy and a higher level of political awareness among most people. Even dictatorships today frequently employ token elections to at least give the appearance of popular support for their regimes. In many ways it is becoming increasingly difficult, Afzaal argues, for modern nation-states to govern an uncooperative populace, meaning that nonviolent forms of resistance that withdraw consent and cooperation "have now become immensely powerful means for changing and reforming social structures and institutions."[14] Afzaal wrote this prior to the Arab Spring. His ideas seem prescient in light of the largely nonviolent overthrow of the Mubarak regime in Egypt in 2011. It should not be surprising that Afzaal is a student of both Gandhi and Martin Luther King Jr., the twin prophets of nonviolent resistance. While he has been influenced by both Hindu and Christian figures, Afzaal's reclaiming of jihad as fundamental for Muslim identity, and his reinterpretation of jihad as a *nonviolent* struggle for justice is a critical message for Muslim ears.

Qutb and Afzaal have much to teach us about jihad and its fundamental importance for Muslim identity. But beyond Muslim scholars, we might also consider those who have put jihad into action in a way consistent with the highest ideals of Islam. I can think of no better example in this regard than the Emir Abd el-Kader.

Emir Abd el-Kader

About an hour south of my home in Decorah, Iowa, lies the small town of Elkader. Founded along the banks of the Turkey River, Elkader was named by its founder, Timothy Davis, after the nineteenth-century Algerian military leader Emir Abd el-Kader. Why would the founder of a small town in rural Iowa in the 1840s name his new settlement after an Algerian? And if this Algerian was so famous in the 1840s to become the eponymous

14. Ibid., 23.

inspiration for a small Iowa settlement, why has the name Abd el-Kader completely dropped out of the American lexicon to the point that even many residents of Elkader would be hard pressed today to explain the origin of their town's name? The first question is easy to answer, the second less so. But the Emir Abd el-Kader was such an extraordinary individual that some people in Elkader have recently teamed up with the author of a contemporary biography of the emir[15] to found the Abd el-Kader Education Project, an initiative designed to recover the example of Emir Abd el-Kader as a positive role model for people today. A centerpiece of this project is an essay contest for high school and college students, designed to inspire young people to lives of service and interfaith understanding and respect, following the example of the emir's life. So what was so extraordinary about this individual?

Emir Abd el-Kader rose to prominence in Algeria during the colonial occupation of his country by French forces beginning in the 1830s. Raised to live the quiet life of a religious scholar highly influenced by the esoteric Sufi form of Islam, Abd el-Kader was thrust into military leadership mostly against his will. He accepted the task and more than proved himself up to the challenge. In response to the French invasion, a jihad was declared to defend Algeria against this foreign threat and Abd el-Kader successfully marshaled the fractious tribes of Algerian society and melded them into an effective fighting force that provided a strong source of resistance to the superior French military. However, Abd el-Kader distinguished himself not only by his military and political acumen but also by his humanity in the face of a brutal enemy.

French colonial invasions into North Africa in the nineteenth century were justified on the grounds that the French were bringing the light of civilization to barbaric Arab tribes. Extremely violent tactics were authorized as part of this "civilizing" project. An 1883 French Government Inquiry Commission report admits that

> We massacred people carrying [French] passes, on a suspicion we slit the throats of entire populations who were later on proven to be innocent; we tried men famous for the holiness in the land, venerated men, because they had enough courage to come and meet our rage in order to intercede on behalf of their fellow

---

15. See Kiser, *Commander of the Faithful.* In addition, two works have been produced: an intellectual and spiritual biography—Bouyerdene, *Emir Abd el-Kader*—and a biography specifically for teenage readers—Marston, *Compassionate Warrior.*

countrymen; there were men to sentence them and civilized men to have them executed.[16]

What was Abd el-Kader's response to such brutal tactics? Given that the emir's military effort had the official status of a jihad, and given the images we associate with jihad today, we might expect that Frenchmen who fell into the hands of Abd el-Kader's men would have been brutalized. But the truth is entirely contrary.

Abd el-Kader refused to stoop to the level of his "civilized" French adversaries and instead treated French prisoners with the utmost dignity, an action that won him great respect among the French generals. Abd el-Kader completely exploded the myth of barbarian Arab tribes by basing his jihad on principles of human dignity that embarrassed his rivals, a point emphasized by his first biographer, Charles H. Churchill:

> The generous concern, the tender sympathy, shown by Abd el-Kader to his prisoners, are almost without parallel in the annals of war. The Christian generals on this point do not reach his ankles and may well blush at the degradation of their sentiments of humanity. To be sure, it cannot be denied that the prisoners taken by the Arabs were often exposed to insults of their barbaric vanquishers, when they fell into the midst of tribes exasperated by the sufferings inflicted upon them by the French. However, slowly but surely, the spirit breathed by the Sultan made its way. Barbarism withdrew before him, charity emerged, humanity triumphed.[17]

These actions of Emir Abd el-Kader stand in stark contrast to the treatment of prisoners both by contemporary jihadists, who have terrorized and killed Western journalists (like Daniel Pearl), and by the American military, which has tortured and denigrated the dignity of Islamic militants in places like Abu Ghraib and Guantánamo. We all have much to learn from the emir!

With military and political skill, an iron will, and a spirit grounded firmly in a life of submission to God, Emir Abd el-Kader successfully resisted French incursions for nearly seventeen years. Ultimately, however, he was forced to abandon the jihad and he reluctantly surrendered to French forces in 1847. He, his family, and his closest associates were taken to France to live in exile. During this time, the emir became something of a sensation

16. Quoted in Shah-Khazemi, "From the Spirituality of *Jihad* to the Ideology of Jihadism," 131.

17. Quoted in Bouyerdene, *Emir Abd el-Kader*, 102.

within the elite circles of French society, and he developed relationships of mutual respect with prominent leaders, especially with members of the Roman Catholic hierarchy. He engaged in deep theological discussions with Catholic clerics, developing a deep respect for Christianity and for the society that had brutally invaded his homeland. If this was all the emir's fame rested on it would be enough, but the story does not end here.

Abd el-Kader had a strong desire to return to the Arab world to live out his days. The French, of course, would not allow a return to Algeria. But they did finally agree to send him to Damascus. There, Abd el-Kader along with his family and associates were settled in a rather large compound with a generous pension. The emir could finally settle down to the life of quiet contemplation and scholarship he had always coveted. But in 1860, violence broke out in Damascus in the form of an anti-Christian pogrom. Muslims and Druze rioted in the city slaughtering any Christian they could identify. Abd el-Kader—who had unsuccessfully tried to broker a peace deal—and his men sprang into action, rounding up Christians in the streets and conveying them to the Abd el-Kader residence for protection. At great risk to his own life, Abd el-Kader is credited with saving many thousands of Christian lives. It was this selfless action that cemented Abd el-Kader's global reputation. He was hailed by the queen of England, the pope, and Abraham Lincoln (who sent him two Colt pistols as a gift). Upon his death in 1883, The *New York Times* hailed him as "one of the few great men of the century."

Reflecting on the life of this true hero, Ahmed Bouyerdene writes:

> Abd el-kader was led by an idea of brotherhood which viewed the other, whether familiar or stranger, a fellow creature, another "me." During the war, he had treated the French prisoners like his own soldiers. In Damascus, he had risked his life to save Christians out of humanity. In the letters written in captivity, he addresses family and strangers in the same manner: the same formulas of civility, the same religious references, the same prayers, with the persistent will of treating one and all on the same footing of equality. Muslims and non-Muslims, all believers, above and beyond all dogmatic differences, are "brothers," including those whose function placed them in the position of adversaries.[18]

The example of Emir Abd el-Kader is truly inspiring and raises the bar of what it means to be human for all of us. It is not difficult to see why John

18. Quoted in ibid., 189.

W. Kiser has dubbed his life "A Story of True Jihad." But if Abd el-Kader's life is an example of "true jihad," it raises the troubling question of what has happened to jihad (and therefore the prophetic spirit of Islam) in our own times.

THE FAILURE OF JIHAD IN CONTEMPORARY ISLAM

If we survey the Muslim world today, examples like Emir Abd el-Kader are becoming increasingly hard to find. The humanity with which he waged jihad is being replaced in too many cases with a barbarism completely at odds with traditional Islamic sources. Whether it is al-Qaeda's jihad against America and its Western allies or the jihad of Hamas or Hizbollah against Israel and its American backers, respect for the dignity of human life has been replaced with the wanton slaughter of innocents, including children, without any clear strategic or moral intent. The Western world's colonial domination of the Muslim world and its natural resources (mostly oil) is an enormous injustice, and it certainly needs to be resisted. Israel's occupation of Palestinian territories and its ghettoization and indiscriminate killing of the people of Gaza must also be resisted. But flying airplanes into tall buildings and blowing up buses with suicide bombers does not even begin to address these injustices, nor is it consistent with the Islamic affirmation of the dignity of all human life, even the lives of those who do wrong. Terrorism is not jihad.

Just imagine what might happen if the leaders of Hamas developed an Abd el-Kader-like attitude toward the Israeli people, refusing to respond to the barbarism of the Israeli occupation with the equal barbarism of killing innocent Israeli citizens. Just imagine the leaders of Hamas developing an interest in and appreciation for the culture and religion of this brutal occupying force the way Abd el-Kader developed respect for the French Christians who had brutalized the people of Algeria. Just imagine the leaders of Hamas in a (hopefully) hypothetical future intervening to save the lives of Israelis being slaughtered by Iranian forces. Alternatively, what if the Israeli government refused to stoop to the level of Hamas, and returned Hamas rocket fire with humanitarian aid to the Palestinian people? Or what if American Christians intervened to save the lives of Muslims in some hypothetical future anti-Muslim pogrom? You can't imagine any of these scenarios? It's hard, I admit. Such scenarios may have even been beyond the ability of John Lennon to imagine. And yet, just over a century ago, a similar scenario played out in the life of Emir Abd el-Kader, so these scenarios cannot be considered impossible. What is different today?

Abd el-Kader was steeped in the spiritual traditions of Islam as he had absorbed them from his Sufi upbringing. He was firmly grounded in a life of submission to a divine entity more real to him than virtually anything else in his life. Listen to his own words as he describes the motivating force for his selfless act of saving the Christians of Damascus. In response to a letter of congratulations he writes:

> You are mistaken in congratulating me: I do not deserve it, for in the midst of these events I was merely an instrument. Send your praises to Him who directed me, to your Sultan and mine. When I advanced through the streets of Damascus, I was seeing Him walking before me. He would tell me: 'do this,' and I did it; 'go this way,' and I went, 'save this man,' and I saved him. Thus, I did naught but obey, and obedience does not justify the praises you bestow upon me; they all belong to Him who commanded.[19]

Such depth of spirituality, such depth of contact with the reality of the divine, seems missing from those whose jihad devolves into a superficial game of retaliation. Islamic terrorist networks in the contemporary world act more like the tribal polytheists of pre-Islamic Arabia—defending honor through unending spirals of retaliatory violence—and less like Muhammad when he refused to slaughter the people of Mecca upon his triumphant return to the city that had tried to kill him. Authentic jihad cannot be separated from its spiritual moorings without devolving into a set of strategies and tactics devoid of any sense of the dignity of all human life. (American foreign and military policy has also become unmoored from any deeper moral intelligence; this is not a problem restricted to Islamic terrorists.)

But most Muslims are not terrorists. Most Muslims do not declare jihad against supposed infidels. Most Muslims consider themselves peaceful adherents of the religion of Islam. Far more troubling than the corruption of authentic jihad by Islamic terrorists is the complete loss of any sense of the importance of jihad among the vast majority of the world's Muslims. Jihad has gone AWOL.

There are two main reasons for this "missing jihad." First, as Western secularism has been spread abroad through the process of globalization, Islam has been religionized. That is, this rich tradition of societal transformation is placed in the safe category called religion where it devolves

19. Quoted in ibid., 121.

to a set of beliefs and practices addressing the spiritual lives of individuals, effectively neutralizing its larger political thrust. If one prays, worships, fasts, and practices the Five Pillars, one is a good, pious Muslim. A religionized Islam has little relevance for systems of political or economic injustice, and so there is no need for religious, nonprophetic Muslims to engage in the struggle for social transformation. This is just the situation that those embrace who benefit from the unjust status quo. The sacred/secular conceptual dichotomy, as I argued earlier, creates the conditions for the development of unjust economic systems. So, as long as religion can be conceptually split off from a secular realm, and Islam can be placed firmly on the religion side of this dichotomy, jihad loses all significance as a fundamental part of an Islamic worldview, and calls for jihad become branded, ironically, as a corruption of the authentic, peaceful religion of Islam—as a corrupt politicizing of Islam. The problem, however, isn't that Islam today is too political. On the contrary, it is the religionizing of Islam that represents the corrupting influence.[20]

Along with this religionized domestication of Islam, we also find an Islamophobic rhetorical strategy at work that so effectively caricatures Islam as an inherently violent force of world domination that rank-and-file Muslims feel compelled to adopt an Islam-is-peace discourse, thereby intentionally distancing themselves from any association with a term carrying the negative valence that *jihad* carries in the West. South African Muslim scholar Farid Esack has critiqued what he calls a form of "liberal Islam" that emerged after the 9/11 attacks. Not wanting to be associated with terrorists, many Muslim intellectuals adopted an apologetic stance whereby Islam was conceived as a source for peace and prosperity, not violence and backwardness.

But Esack, who eschews the label "liberal Muslim" and refers to himself instead as a progressive Muslim, finds much to fault in this otherwise understandable apologetic move:

> While progressive Muslims shared the revulsion of others at the death of innocents, they display a much more cynical attitude towards an uncritiqued peace discourse. For progressive Muslims,

20. The ignorance of this even among Muslims is on full display in the recent book by Muslim political scientist Bassam Tibi, *Islamism and Islam*. Tibi views Islamism, of which he is highly critical, as a modern form of "religionized politics" and as completely distinct from the apolitical religion of Islam, of which he is a proponent. For Tibi, the apolitical religion of Islam preserves the spirit of the historical Islamic tradition, with Islamism serving as a specifically modern aberration. He seems to have it backward!

"real peace" seems to be one that follows the creation of a just world. In contrast, a seemingly ideology-less peace that, uncritiqued, translates into acquiescence to a new corporate dominated world—most starkly represented by the United States of America—is one to be not only avoided but opposed. Dominant empires develop an ideological rooted interest in peace which reinforces a *status quo* that may very well be an unjust one.[21]

While Esack does not disagree in principle that Islam should be a force for peace in the world, true peace for him will only accompany the development of a just world. To be a force for peace, Islam must be a force willing to disrupt the unjust status quo when necessary. And any attempt to disrupt the status quo will always entail a struggle, a jihad. Those whom Esack calls "liberal Muslims"—cowed into submission by the powerful stereotype of a scary, violent Islam—have essentially given up on jihad entirely, or have reinterpreted it as a fully internal, individualistic spiritual struggle (like the MyJihad Campaign). Whether the concept of jihad is drowned out by uncritical pace discourse or individualized and spiritualized, the prophetic voice of Islam is effectively silenced.

Whether it results from the barbarism of a spiritually superficial Islam of retaliatory violence, or from the political impotence of a liberal apologetic Islam of personal piety, an authentic spirit of jihad is quickly disappearing from the Islamic tradition and with it a much needed prophetic voice. There can be no prophetic voice absent a robust and spiritually grounded conception of jihad, for jihad is, almost by definition, the lynchpin of a prophetic Islam. Where the struggle disappears to transform worldly structures and institutions so that they reflect and spread greater levels of justice and peace, we find an Islam that acquiesces to systems of injustice and oppression—a decidedly unprophetic Islam. This desperately needs to change, and ironically, one of the ways it could change is through a recovery of the prophetic figure standing at the heart of the Christian (and to a great extent also the Islamic) tradition—Jesus. The life and work of Jesus may indeed be an example of jihad at its best. It is time to explore the central theme of this book, summed up in its title: *Jesus and Jihad.*

21. Esack, "In Search of Progressive Islam beyond 9/11," 84.

4

Jesus and Jihad

Has anyone been misunderstood as Jesus has?

—WALTER RAUSCHENBUSCH

According to a contemporary Muslim scholar, Amin Ahsan Islahi,

> It is on record that the Prophet Jesus (peace and blessings be upon him) exhorted his disciples to wage *Jihad*. The same call was given by all the Messengers.[1]

Obviously, the Jesus/jihad connection at the heart of this book's argument is uncontroversial among Muslims. Because Jesus's prophetic status figures so prominently in the Islamic tradition, the idea that he "struggled in the way of God" is simply taken for granted. For Muslims, Jesus himself was a muslim (one who lives a life of submission to God), and engaging in jihad, as we have seen, is simply what muslims (and Muslims) are called to do.

Though the Jesus/jihad connection may be uncontroversial among Muslims, the same cannot be said for Christians. Equating the savior of humanity with an idea as detested in the West as jihad will seem heretical to many Christians (and I'm sure I'll hear about it, especially from those who refuse to take the time to actually read this book!). But if you have read

1. Islahi, "Self-Development," 201.

this far, you know that *jihad* is a term used to describe the struggle to bring about a world of justice and peace lived in reference to divine sovereignty. Equating Jesus with jihad, then, is not an act that denigrates Jesus at all; it is rather a high compliment! If Christians can get beyond a knee-jerk rejection of the Jesus/jihad connection and open to the possibility that they might have much to learn from a Muslim understanding of Jesus, then this book will have accomplished one of its primary goals.

But even in this rosy scenario, there will remain the issue that Jesus is viewed by many as a spiritual figure who died for the sins of humanity so that those who believe in him might not die but inherit eternal life. Even if we buy into an understanding of jihad as a movement of social transformation toward greater levels of justice, we may still balk at the association of Jesus with jihad simply because we resist viewing Jesus in such an overtly political way. Jesus in the West is a religious figure relevant primarily to the spiritual lives of individuals. Seeing him as an activist for social, political, and economic change almost transforms him into a 1960s hippie-like figure, an image that won't sit well with the conservative political and religious establishment. (All the paintings *do* portray Jesus with long hair!) But the Jesus of personal piety has little historical evidence to support it. I am convinced that the Jesus/jihad connection, beyond its beautiful alliterative quality, also makes good historical sense. True, the Gospels nowhere portray Jesus as specifically exhorting his disciples on to jihad. (How could they? Jesus didn't speak Arabic!) But given the understanding of jihad we developed in the last chapter and what we have come to understand about the nature of Jesus's ministry in recent years, the Jesus/jihad association is entirely appropriate, predictable Christian protestations to it notwithstanding.

Recall from our discussion in chapter 2 that religion, conceived as a unique sphere of human life distinct from the so-called secular sphere of politics and economics, is a modern Western (and largely Christian) idea. New Testament Greek has no word for *religion*. The sacred/secular dichotomy so familiar to us in the West would likely have sounded foreign to the ears of Jesus and his contemporaries. Almost by definition, Jesus's original followers could not have viewed him as a religious figure. So how did they understand him? Recent years have witnessed a sea change in New Testament studies as scholars are reinterpreting Jesus's life and ministry in a way that takes seriously the realities of Roman imperial domination of subject peoples. The results of this reinterpretation are startling, and once understood can only be characterized as consistent with the Islamic concept of jihad. If you have never before thought of Jesus as a highly political figure, the following discussion might seem rather jarring at first. But the evidence cannot be ignored. It is time to make explicit the clear connection between Jesus and jihad.

ROMAN IMPERIALISM IN JUDEA AND GALILEE

Jesus lived in a time and place indelibly influenced by the harsh realities of the Roman imperial system. With the accession of Caesar Augustus to the Roman throne in 30 BCE, the Roman Empire was launched into a period of unparalleled peace and prosperity known as the *Pax Romana*. As warring factions and internecine strife were replaced by Augustus's grand unification of the Roman world, economic activity expanded to such an extent that wealth poured into the imperial center (the city of Rome), wealth that could then be used to further expand the boundaries of the empire. Jesus, therefore, lived during a time of great peace and prosperity, which seems like a good thing until we realize that this prosperity was not shared by those deemed subjects of the empire—the vast majority of the empire's population. The *Pax Romana* was, to be sure, a benefit to the Roman elite, but it was experienced as anything but peace by the Jewish community of first-century Roman Palestine of which Jesus was a part.

The wealth of Rome was bought on the backs of the exploited poor. The imperial elite (roughly 2–3 percent of the empire's population) owned most of the land, which they leased out to tenant farmers who provided the labor. The vast majority of the land's productivity, however, went directly into the pockets of the wealthy landowners, not into the pockets of the peasants who worked the land; the peasants were left to struggle for subsistence. It is the very purpose of empire to funnel resources and wealth from conquered peoples into the imperial center, and this requires the empire to maintain exploitative economic relationships with the people of the lands they occupy. Rome was the empire par excellence. Rome had raised the process of exploitation to a science, which is why they were one of the most powerful empires to ever grace the surface of the earth.[2]

A high degree of political stability was required to keep the imperial economic machinery humming. Major disruptions along trade and transportation routes would have negative economic impacts, and so (not

2. See, e.g., Oakman, *Jesus and the Peasants*; and Horsley, *Jesus and Empire*.

surprisingly) the Roman Empire invested tremendous resources in the development of a frighteningly efficient military apparatus to police the supply lines and trade routes. The Roman legions were deployed primarily to intimidate the population into submission. Any attempt to disrupt the imperial system was quickly and brutally crushed. In fact, the use of crucifixion as a means of execution was probably developed for just this purpose: there are certainly much quicker and more efficient ways to execute those deemed a threat to the empire than to let them hang on crosses for days on end. Beheading would have been much faster (and more humane). But the Romans did not seek to merely execute those it deemed a threat; they desired to intimidate the subject populations in order to ward off any possible future threats. Crucifixion was a terrible way to die: the unfortunate victim had to choose between (on the one hand) suffocating and (on the other hand) pushing the body upward just to breathe, and this meant putting one's weight on feet driven through with nails the size of railroad spikes. By making this torturous method of execution a public spectacle, the Romans sent the message in no uncertain terms that resistance to the imperial system would be met with inhumane brutality.

The Judean historian Josephus provides us with great insight into the conditions of life endured by the Jewish subjects of the empire. I want to draw on three examples that illustrate the great difficulties inherent in being an imperial subject. The first concerns the exploits of a Jewish shepherd named Athrongaeus. Athrongaeus, we are told, placed a crown upon his head and aspired to a life of royalty. Raising a band of men, he led his followers into raids on Roman convoys carrying supplies to military troops in the field. In one case, Athrongaeus and his men killed a centurion and forty of his soldiers. But they must have enjoyed other successes as well because Josephus claims that "at the period of which we are speaking, these men were making the whole of Judaea one scene of guerilla warfare."[3]

The empire, of course, would not sit idly by and accept this kind of disruption to the imperial system. Very quickly, then, Athrongaeus and his followers were either captured or killed. This should have put an end to the whole affair, but the Romans were not done. In order to intimidate the population into submission, the Roman general Varus went on a rampage, killing all those who opposed him, then burning to the ground the entire city of Sepphoris, a town along the Sea of Galilee, not far from Nazareth.

3. Thackeray, trans., Josephus, *Jewish War* 2.65. See Horsley and Hanson, *Bandits, Prophets, and Messiahs.*

There is no evidence that Athrongaeus had any connection to Sepphoris. But the point here is that to the Roman elite, the people of Judea and Galilee were expendable. They enjoyed no status in the imperial system, so they could be wantonly slaughtered simply as a show of intimidation even if innocent of any wrongdoing. The imperial system was brutal. This whole affair occurred within a few years of Jesus's birth. During Jesus's childhood, the people of nearby Nazareth would still have had fresh memories of this carnage.

Our second illustration of the hardships of life under imperial domination concerns the familiar figure of Pontius Pilate. Pilate, of course, was the procurator of Judea at the time of Jesus's crucifixion. The Gospels portray him as being a rather wishy-washy figure: the Jewish crowds bully him into crucifying Jesus even though he finds Jesus to be innocent of any wrongdoing. But Josephus's portrait is altogether different. We are told that Pilate wanted to build an aqueduct to bring water from a distance of four hundred furlongs into the city. To finance this civil project, Pilate raided the temple treasury, withdrawing money that had been dedicated to God by the Jewish people. Indignant at this offense against their religious sensibilities, an angry Jewish mob besieged Pilate, who just happened to be on a visit to Jerusalem. But Pilate was prepared for the public outcry and had interspersed among the crowd soldiers disguised as civilians. Upon receiving a signal from Pilate, the soldiers pulled out cudgels and began beating the Jewish crowds mercilessly. Josephus relates that large numbers of Jews were killed, both from the blows they received and from being trodden to death as the panicked crowds fled.

Pilate clearly knew that raiding the temple treasury to build an aqueduct would provoke an angry response. And in some ways it seems he did this on purpose in order to stir up the crowds so that he could turn on them violently. In fact, records show that Pilate was later recalled to Rome specifically because he had done such a poor job of maintaining peace and stability. But as with the previous example, so we see here again how little regard Roman officials had for their Jewish subjects, whose lives were considered expendable. We see also how the temple in Jerusalem actually functioned. It was a Roman bank. Roman officials worked closely with the temple priests to maintain a system whereby the Jewish people would be socialized into the necessity of bringing offerings to God. As money flowed into the temple, the Romans had a ready source of funds for their own imperial projects. In this case, religious sensibilities brilliantly led the people to willingly participate in their own exploitation. I will have more to say about this important dynamic below.

Our third example comes from a somewhat later time, the governorship of Cumanus (48–52 CE). As was customary, a large crowd had descended on Jerusalem to celebrate Passover. Given that Passover is a commemoration of the liberation of the Israelite people from slavery in Egypt, Roman officials became very nervous about large Jewish crowds streaming into Jerusalem to celebrate salvation from a foreign oppressor. Not surprisingly, then, the Romans placed a cohort of visibly armed soldiers in and around the temple area to intimidate the crowds and quell any thought of fomenting a rebellion. The scene was probably similar to one I experienced some years ago in Turkey. I had stumbled upon a protest march in a public square. Soon I realized that a large number of police fitted out in full riot gear had assembled along the storefronts, ready to forcibly quell any disturbances. Back in the first century, Josephus relates that a Roman cohort had taken up a position on the roof of the portico of the temple, when

> one of the soldiers, raising his robe, stooped in an indecent attitude, so as to turn his backside to the Jews, and made a noise in keeping with his posture. Enraged by this insult, the whole multitude with loud cries called upon Cumanus to punish the soldier; some of the more hot-headed young men and seditious persons in the crowd started a fight, and, picking up stones, hurled them at the troops.[4]

Fearing a general breakdown of order, Cumanus called in reinforcements who sealed off all escape routes leaving the panicked crowd to be trampled to death in the ensuing melee. Josephus claims that upwards of thirty thousand people died, though this number is probably an exaggeration. Still, this story illustrates well just how tense the relations were between the Roman elite and their Jewish subjects. A simple, well-timed, crude act of disrespect could provoke a tragic riot.

Many more examples like this exist in the literature, but these should suffice to make the point; life under the yoke of Roman power was, to borrow a phrase used by the philosopher Thomas Hobbes to characterize premodern existence, "nasty, brutish, and short." The Romans were not benevolent rulers; they were a brutally violent occupying force with no regard for the suffering of subject peoples. This was the context in which Jesus's life and ministry played out. Did Jesus stand idly by in the face of oppression

---

4. Thackeray, trans., Josephus, *Jewish War* 2.224.

and injustice and preach a spiritual message of individual salvation, as many Christians today seem to believe? Or did he take a prophetic stand against the injustice and wage a jihad to try and transform it? The evidence overwhelmingly indicates that Jesus did the latter.

JESUS AND ROME

Christians have traditionally treated the Roman Empire as a neutral backdrop against which the religious mission of Jesus played out, as if the ministry of Jesus and the realities of Roman imperial rule constituted trains running along parallel tracks. But as we have just seen, nothing could be further from the truth. Roman imperial rule was not experienced as neutral by its subjects; it rather colored every aspect of the lives of Jesus and his contemporaries, though it is only in recent years that New Testament scholars have opened fully to this reality and begun to reinterpret the Gospels in light of it. It is virtually impossible for Jesus to have said and done the things he is portrayed as having said and done without provoking imperial suspicions. Jesus and Rome were not trains running on parallel tracks but trains hurtling toward each other on a collision course. Jesus's whole mission revolved around prophetic resistance to Roman exploitation; his message was manifestly not one of personal spirituality. Let's reread some of the familiar texts from the Gospels with this prophetic Jesus in mind.

Birth Narratives

The first hint that Jesus's mission would be prophetic and profoundly political comes in the familiar song known as the Magnificat, sung by his mother Mary in the opening pages of Luke's gospel:

> My soul magnifies the Lord,
>   and my spirit rejoices in God my Savior,
> for he has looked with favor on the lowliness of his servant.
>   Surely, from now on all generations will call me blessed;
> for the Mighty One has done great things for me,
>   and holy is his name.
> His mercy is for those who fear him
>   from generation to generation.
> He has shown strength with his arm;
>   he has scattered the proud in the thoughts of their hearts.

> He has brought down the powerful from their thrones,
>> and lifted up the lowly;
> he has filled the hungry with good things,
>> and sent the rich away empty. (Luke 1:47–53)

According to Mary, the baby in her womb will bring about nothing less than the complete inversion of the socioeconomic order of the empire. The powerful will be brought down from their thrones and the lowly will be lifted up. The rich will be sent away empty while the hungry will be fed. In the context of first-century Palestine, the rich and powerful sitting on thrones can only be a reference to the Roman elite while the lowly are clearly their Jewish subjects. Mary does not predict that Jesus will foment a spiritual revolution in the lives of individuals but that he will engineer a political revolution to transform the unjust status quo of Roman imperial rule into a future of justice and peace. Jesus, she predicts, will wage a jihad.

Having stated it explicitly, Luke then carries this theme through the rest of his narrative of Jesus's birth. Consider the familiar Christmas scene where Jesus is born in a stable in Bethlehem. Angels appear to shepherds on a hillside to announce the birth of a savior:

> In that region there were shepherds living in the fields, keeping watch over their flock by night. Then an angel of the Lord stood before them, and the glory of the Lord shone around them, and they were terrified. But the angel said to them, "Do not be afraid; for see—I am bringing you *good news* [*euangelion* in Greek] of great joy for all the people: to you is born this day in the city of David a *Savior*, who is the *Messiah*, the Lord." (Luke 2:8–12, italics added)

It may be tempting to interpret terms like "good news," "Savior," and "Messiah" in pietistic ways, hearing the angel's words as a proclamation of salvation from individual sin. But such a reading completely misses the strong political resonances apparent here to anyone familiar with Roman realities; and the original readers of Luke's Gospel would know these realities all too well!

Tradition says that Jesus was born sometime around the year 4 BCE. If this is right, then his birth was only a few years removed from the writing of a Greek inscription found among the ruins of the city of Priene in Asia Minor (present-day Turkey). Dated to 9 BCE, this inscription celebrates the birthday of the Roman emperor Caesar Augustus, the creator of the Pax

Romana. Listen to the language used to describe what Caesar meant to the people of Rome:

> Whereas Providence, which has regulated our whole existence, has brought our life to the climax of perfection in giving to us Augustus, whom it [Providence] filled with strength for the welfare of men, and who being sent to us and our descendents as a *Savior*, has put an end to war and has set all things in order; and having become manifest, Caesar has fulfilled all the hopes of earlier times in surpassing all the benefactors who preceded him, and whereas, finally, the birthday of the god has been for the whole world the beginning of *good news* [*euangelion* in Greek] concerning him, therefore let a new era begin from his birth.[5]

The parallels with Luke's description of the birth of Jesus are striking. The Priene Inscription (written before Jesus was born) is demonstrably older than Luke's gospel. So in using terms like *savior* and *good news*, it is clear that Luke has intentionally co-opted the very language of Roman imperial theology and applied it to a humble baby lying in a manger.

The message could not be more powerful. Augustus's coming was not *good news* for the world but only for the small group of Roman elite who enjoyed the benefits of empire. Augustus may have been experienced as a *savior*, but he saved only the same small group of Roman elites, not the subjects of the imperial system. In fact, it is the imperial subjects who need salvation from the oppressive effects of imperial power. And Luke has the audacity to suggest that it is this little baby wrapped in swaddling clothes who will do what the powerful Roman emperor (who was worshipped as a god) will not do—create a just and equitable society for all the people of the earth. When the angels announce the birth of a Savior to the shepherds on the hillside, they are announcing the coming of the one who will save them from Roman power, not individual sin. This is a prophetic—and very political—message.

Luke is not alone in portraying the birth of Jesus in an overtly political and anti-Roman way. Matthew has his own version of Jesus's birth. It may be very different from Luke's in the details, but the overall effect is very much the same: Jesus is a threat to Roman imperial power. In Matthew, Jesus's birth, which does not occur in a stable, is portrayed as the birth of a king, a king of the Jews, to be specific. Wise men from the east come to him bearing royal gifts of gold, frankincense, and myrrh, and prostrate

5. Translation adapted from that cited in Horsley, *Jesus and Empire*, 23 (italics added).

themselves before him in worship. The problem is that the Roman puppet king, Herod, is, technically, king of the Jews, and he will brook no rivals. Herod, therefore, immediately recognizes the birth of Jesus as a threat to his sovereignty and concocts a scheme to eliminate this disturbing rival. We are so familiar with this story that we fail to see how ridiculous it really is. A powerful king backed by the most powerful empire the world had ever known is afraid of a baby born to a poor peasant couple in the backwater village of Bethlehem? Really? No, not really. This is obviously not a historical recounting. It is simply Matthew's way of indicating that Jesus's later ministry must be understood as having a strong anti-imperial dimension. In Matthew's story a Roman puppet king recognizes Jesus's status as a political threat right from his birth.

The birth narratives of Matthew and Luke both portray Jesus as a figure who would grow up to lead a movement of resistance to the injustices authorized by the Roman imperial system. How is this portrayed later in the Gospels? One way is through the familiar title that has come to function for Christians as a kind of last name for Jesus: Messiah (Christ).

Messiah

Of all the titles applied to Jesus, Messiah might be the one most misunderstood by Christians. This misunderstanding has not been helped by the great German composer George Frederick Handel's famous oratorio, *Messiah*, which frames Jesus's identity as the Messiah around an individualistic German piety in a most ironic way. Handel's *Messiah* is obviously all about Jesus. But the oratorio borrows much of its libretto from the prophet Isaiah, seemingly unaware that the only figure actually called Messiah by Isaiah is the Persian king Cyrus (Isa 45:1). Handel was a musical genius to be sure, but he was not much of a biblical scholar! Be that as it may, the term Messiah comes to be equated within the Christian tradition with the idea of a Savior in an individualistic, spiritual sense. But in the first century, Messiah was as political a title as there was.

The term *messiah* occurs frequently in the Hebrew Bible, where it always refers to historical figures. The word means "anointed one," and so is applied to kings and prophets, who were considered to be anointed by God. But of course kings and prophets were very political figures. Kings oversaw the political, economic, and military affairs of the Israelite and Judean kingdoms while prophets frequently acted as advisors to these kings.

As I mentioned above, the title Messiah even gets applied to a Persian king; it is not a title reserved only for Israelite royal figures. It is not until long after the history related in the Hebrew Bible that the term *messiah* comes to be applied to a figure yet to arrive on the scene. Interestingly, this new forward-looking use of the term *messiah* appears in Jewish literature for the first time shortly after 63 BCE, the year that the Roman general Pompey annexed Palestine, bringing the Jewish community back under foreign control following nearly a century of autonomy under the Jewish Hasmonean kings. Jewish messianic expectations appear to have been directly sparked by the harsh realities of life under the Roman military occupation.

Nowhere is this better articulated than in a group of Roman-era Jewish writings known as the *Psalms of Solomon*. The seventeenth psalm lays out in detail the job description of this hoped-for messianic figure:

> See, Lord, and raise up for them their king,
> the son of David, to rule over your servant Israel
> in a time known to you, O God.
> Undergird him with strength to *destroy* the unrighteous rulers,
> to *purge* Jerusalem from gentiles who trample her to destruction;
> in wisdom and in righteousness to *drive out* the sinners from the
> inheritance;
> to *smash* the arrogance of sinners like a potter's jar;
> to *shatter* all their substance with an iron rod;
> to *destroy* the unlawful nations with the word of his mouth.
> At his warning the nations will flee from his presence;
> and he will *condemn* sinners by the thoughts of their hearts . . .
> And he will be a righteous king over them, taught by God.
> There will be no unrighteousness among them in his days,
> for all shall be holy, and their king shall be the Lord Messiah.[6]
> (*PssSol* 17:21–24, 32; italics added)

The language is striking. The Messiah here is assumed to be a king, and one specifically descended from King David (the great military ruler of ancient Israel). This Messiah's job, in short, is to "destroy," "purge," "drive out," "smash," "shatter," "destroy," and "condemn." But who is he supposed to wreak this destruction upon? The answer is explicit: "unrighteous rulers," "gentiles who trample Jerusalem to destruction," "sinners," and "unlawful nations." Given that these psalms were written shortly after the Roman annexation of Palestine, we need not guess to whom these terms refer. Gentiles who trample Jerusalem to destruction are Romans. The Messiah's

---

6. English translation in Wright, "Psalms of Solomon," 667.

mission is nothing short of the utter destruction of the Roman Empire. The Messiah is a militant, explicitly anti-Roman, figure.

Now Jesus quite obviously did not fulfill these longings for the destruction of the empire. But if it is true, as the Gospels attest, that the title Messiah was being applied to him by his followers, then Jesus must have been involved in activity that at least raised the hopes of his followers for an imminent end to the empire. Such expectations are clear in the Palm Sunday episode where Jesus arrives in Jerusalem on a donkey with crowds of people shouting, "Hosanna to the Son of David!" Hosanna was a cry of pleading which meant roughly, "Save us now!" What did the people need to be saved from? Roman military occupation and economic exploitation, of course. They were desperate for help, knew that the Messiah was the answer, and believed (wrongly) that Jesus was about to fulfill those violent messianic expectations. The only way they could have developed those kinds of expectations about Jesus is if Jesus himself was engaged in some type of anti-Roman activity, even if it did not rise to the level of complete destruction of the empire. Traces of Jesus's involvement in anti-Roman activity can be found all over the gospels.

The Kingdom of God

Three of the four Gospels—Matthew, Mark, and Luke—portray Jesus proclaiming chiefly the coming of the kingdom of God. In many cases, this proclamation of the coming kingdom is couched in parables designed to demonstrate the characteristics of the kingdom. Christians traditionally interpret this proclamation in terms of individual, pietistic faith. The kingdom of God is understood as a heavenly realm populated by those who have been saved by Jesus and have had their sins forgiven. But this completely ignores the political context in which this proclamation is made.

First, consider the famous Lord's Prayer. (Here is the start of Matthew's rendering in the familiar King James Version.) Jesus instructs his disciples to pray saying,

> Our father, which art in heaven.
>   hallowed be thy name.
> Thy kingdom come, thy will be done,
>   in earth as it is in heaven. (Matt 6:9–10)[7]

7. For the economic context of this famous prayer, see Oakman, *Jesus, Debt, and the Lord's Prayer*.

The Lord's Prayer calls for nothing less than the coming of God's kingdom and the imposition of God's will *on earth*—in the material realm of temporal history. The kingdom is not some immaterial, heavenly realm where people go when they die. The coming of the kingdom of God, according to this beloved prayer, is an event that will transform the earthly realm of human history into a replica of the heavenly realm of justice and peace.

The Greek word translated "kingdom" (*basilea*) really does not denote a particular place or location, a meaning we often ascribe to the English word "kingdom." Rather, *basilea* denotes an idea: the idea of sovereignty. The proclamation of the coming of the kingdom of God is the affirmation that a time is rapidly approaching when God's divine sovereignty will rule over the entire earth—a time when all things will be done according to the divine will. Since Jesus consistently casts the coming of divine sovereignty as a future event, he is implying that divine sovereignty does not rule the world during his time. So who *is* ruling the world if God is not? The answer is clear: Caesar.

The Roman Empire claimed for itself absolute sovereignty over land, sea, and the entire earth. The emperors were worshiped as gods, and an elaborate imperial theology was developed to justify their claim to be an earthly reflection of the will of the gods. As just one example of imperial theology, consider a series of coins minted by Caesar Augustus just prior to the Battle of Actium. The six silver *denarii* were struck in two sets of three. In one set, Caesar's head graces the front side of each coin, and the full image of a goddess appears on the reverse. In the other set, Caesar's image is on the back, and a goddess figure is on the front. The message of these images on the *denarii*, of course, is that Caesar is one of the gods. The three goddess figures found on the coins are described by New Testament scholar John Dominic Crossan as "Peace holding her cornucopia of plenty, Venus playing seductively with the armor of Mars, and winged Victory standing on the globe. Roman imperial theology is not just about Italy or even the Mediterranean. It is . . . about the world, the earth, and all its peoples."[8] Each coin also bears the Latin inscription CAESAR DIVI F., meaning "Caesar, son of the deified one." Augustus was the adopted son of Julius Caesar, so Julius is here being represented as a divine figure, and Augustus is the son of a god. We see this also on a Greek beam inscription (once part of a

8. Crossan, "Roman Imperial Theology," 66.

temple in western Turkey), which reads, "To the Imperator Caesar, the Son of God, the God Augustus."[9]

Through coins, inscriptions, and artwork, the message is abundantly clear. Rome was a divine gift to all the earth, and all power and authority had been bestowed on Rome by the gods to rule over all peoples. The kingdom of God had been temporarily supplanted by the kingdom of Caesar. But Jesus has the audacity to proclaim that this situation is not permanent. There cannot be two sovereign powers presiding over the world. Authority cannot be shared. If the kingdom of God is coming, as Jesus proclaims, the kingdom of Caesar will have to be destroyed in the process. It can't be any other way. Jesus's proclamation of a coming kingdom of God could only have been interpreted as a rejection of Roman claims to sovereignty. To proclaim the coming of the kingdom of God in this environment was a highly prophetic—and very subversive—act.

Nowhere is this better demonstrated than in one of the more enigmatic parables Jesus tells to describe the kingdom:

> With what can we compare the kingdom of God, or what parable will we use for it? It is like a grain of mustard seed, which, when sown upon the ground, is the smallest of all the seeds on earth; yet when it is sown it grows up and becomes the greatest of all shrubs, and puts forth large branches, so that the birds of the air can make nests in its shade. (Mark 4:30–32)

What does it mean to compare the kingdom of God to a mustard seed? Does Jesus merely mean to imply that the kingdom will start small and seem insignificant but will eventually become large? Perhaps. But there is likely much more to this. John Dominic Crossan has observed that the first-century Roman writer Pliny the Elder comments on mustard in his multivolume work on the natural history of the Roman Empire. First, Pliny extols the health benefits of mustard and its merits as a cultivated plant, but then warns that mustard is a difficult plant to domesticate because its seeds constantly fall to the ground and germinate so that mustard quickly overtakes anything else growing near it. If you are not careful, Pliny warns, mustard will eventually overrun a fastidiously ordered garden.[10]

Taking Pliny's comments to heart, Crossan suggests a more subversive reading of the parable of the Mustard Seed:

9. Ibid.

10. Rackham, trans., Pliny the Elder, *Natural History* 19.171.

The point, in other words, is not just that the mustard plant starts as a proverbially small seed and grows into a shrub of three or four feet, or even higher, it is that it tends to take over where it is not wanted, that it tends to get out of control, and that it tends to attract birds within cultivated areas where they are not particularly desired. And that, said Jesus, was what the Kingdom was like: not like a mighty cedar of Lebanon and not quite like a common weed, like a pungent shrub with dangerous takeover properties. Something you would only want in small and carefully controlled doses—if you could control it.[11]

In order to maintain the efficient functioning of the Roman imperial system, imperial officials, as we have seen, placed great emphasis on the maintenance of civil order. Recall how Athrongaeus attacked the empire specifically by disrupting supply lines, and how Roman officials placed guards around the temple area during Jewish festivals to intimidate the crowds into maintaining order. The Romans had an almost pathological fixation on maintaining civil order. But Jesus seems to suggest that one of the most important characteristics of the kingdom of God is that it disrupts this order just as mustard disrupts a highly ordered garden. The kingdom of God is subversive; it is a threat to Roman claims of sovereignty.

If Matthew, Mark, and Luke have it right, and Jesus's principal message was to proclaim the advent of a new kingdom, an alternative to the kingdom of Rome, a kingdom of justice and peace presided over by God rather than Caesar, this would have stirred up great hope among the oppressed residents of Palestine and would have made it entirely clear that Jesus's mission was prophetic and political. He was engaged in theologically motivated resistance—jihad—against the imperial forces of occupation, oppression, and injustice.

But what about other aspects of Jesus's mission? Did he not heal people of their diseases? Don't the healing stories simply show Jesus as a compassionate, caring figure responding to people's personal needs? Can the healing accounts be read in a political way too? Indeed they can and they must. To do otherwise is to miss the profound message these healing stories contain.

11. Crossan, *Historical Jesus*, 278.

Jesus's Healings

In the Gospel of John (9:2), Jesus and his disciples come upon a man who has been blind from birth. The disciples instinctively ask Jesus, "Who sinned, this man or his parents that he was born blind?" Jesus rejects his disciples' assumption that the man's infirmity has anything to do with anyone's sin, stating rather that the man was born blind so that the power of God might be revealed in him. Jesus then proceeds to restore the man's sight. Is this just an example of Jesus having compassion on the blind man? Perhaps. But as with the parable of the Mustard Seed, it is so much more. The key here lies in the disciples' question, "Who sinned, this man or his parents, that he was born blind?"

The disciples assume that physical infirmity results from the divine punishment meted out as a result of sin. Those who are disobedient to God will be punished while those who are obedient will prosper. This idea is known as the Deuteronomic view of sin and suffering because it is spelled out in great and gory detail in chapter 28 of the book of Deuteronomy. There we are told that obedience to God will lead to good health, abundant progeny, protection from enemies, and all manner of material prosperity. But disobedience to God will result in physical torment, famine, and an enemy siege so bad that people will be driven to a state of hunger, starvation, and cannibalism (eating their own children, no less!). The point of the Deuteronomic view of suffering is that responsibility for suffering rests in the hands of the person who is suffering. It is the direct result of a person's sin. This Deuteronomic view of suffering meshed well with Roman imperial interests. But what exactly did they gain from it?

The Romans worked closely with the Jewish priesthood that presided over the temple in Jerusalem. One of the temple's main functions was to be a place where atonement for sin could be made. Once a year on the Day of Atonement (or Yom Kippur), the high priest entered the inner sanctum of the temple and made a sacrifice designed to absolve the people of their sins. But beyond this, additional sacrifices and offerings were made throughout the year, all designed to appease a righteous God, and grant salvation from sin. If people could be made to believe that their sufferings and infirmities resulted from their own lack of obedience to God, they would naturally be motivated to bring their offerings to the temple in order to atone for their sin. Money would flow into the temple, creating a ready source of cash that imperial officials could tap for projects that would strengthen the imperial system. Recall the example discussed above of Pilate making a withdrawal, so to speak, from the sacred treasury of the temple in order to build an aqueduct. The temple essentially functioned like a Roman ATM.

This was an ingenious system of imperial exploitation. In many cases the sufferings of Roman subjects were actually the result of institutionalized injustice in the imperial system. But if people could be made to believe their sufferings were rather the result of their own moral failings, they would be less likely to hold the governing powers responsible, and they would be forced to accept "the necessity of an institutionalized system of atonement (sacrifices and offerings) in which God's forgiveness is conditional and is channeled through official mediators and regulators."[12] Such a system kept the people under the control of the temple authorities—the priests—who themselves were just the local representatives of the Roman authorities. What a wonderful way to domesticate a subject population: Get them to willingly participate in their own exploitation! Now, think about the significance of Jesus's healing actions in this context.

First, Jesus rejects the Deuteronomic assumption of the disciples' question, stating that the man's blindness has nothing to do with anyone's sin. Actually, Jesus says, this man was born blind so that God's power could be made manifest directly in the blind man's life. Then Jesus heals him directly. Jesus has the audacity to circumvent the institutional system set up specifically to handle the case of a man with a physical impairment. By healing the man directly, Jesus sends a powerful, and wonderfully subversive, message that God's power is available directly to people. Folks do not need to work through a hierarchical, institutionalized system—one designed specifically for the purposes of imperial exploitation—in order to access divine power. All the healing stories of the Gospels carry with them this subversive political message. Jesus circumvents the imperial system, causing disruptions in the well-oiled machinery of the imperial economy. And we know how well Roman officials tolerated disruption! We can almost hear them crying out, "This Jesus guy is healing people directly rather than sending them to the temple priests for atonement. Such a treasonous action cannot be tolerated!"

Another healing story is even more transparent in its anti-imperial thrust. In chapter 5 of the Gospel of Mark, Jesus and his disciples sail across the Sea of Galilee to the country of the Gerasenes. There they are met by a man with an unclean spirit, who runs around a graveyard howling and bruising himself with stones. The man clearly has a severe mental illness.

12. Horsley, *Jesus and the Spiral of Violence*, 183.

Jesus confronts the man and asks for the name of the unclean spirit possessing him. The spirit replies, "My name is Legion; for we are many." Jesus then proceeds to exorcise the spirits from the man and, at their request, drives them into a herd of swine on the hillside. The demons enter the swine, and the swine then throw themselves off the hillside and into the sea, drowning. Is this just a story of Jesus exorcising demons? Hardly. The demon has a highly suggestive name—Legion—which not coincidentally just happens to be the name for a Roman military unit: the Roman Legions. Jesus has, symbolically at least, driven a legion of the Roman military into the sea.

This story may also be meant to dramatize what happens to people who live under the constant stress of foreign military occupation. You never know when Roman soldiers might come knocking on your door, accusing you of some treasonous act regardless of your guilt or innocence. (Remember what happened to the town of Sepphoris in the Athrongaeus affair.) You have to be careful of everything you say and every action you take because you don't know who might be listening or how your words and actions might be perceived. Living every day in this heightened state of vigilance is extremely stressful and would undoubtedly lead to emotional and mental breakdowns in some people. The man with the unclean spirit is possessed by the Roman military occupation. He regains his sanity only when Jesus drives the Roman legions into the sea. Jesus's healing action is political and prophetic: it is jihad.

Jesus's Crucifixion

All four Gospels portray Jesus's death as a crucifixion. If this is a historical remembrance, then we can only conclude that Jesus was executed by Roman officials for acts of resistance against Roman authority. Crucifixion was a specifically Roman method of execution. As I mentioned above, crucifixion is not an efficient method of execution: bodies could hang on crosses for days as the condemned suffered a slow, agonizing death. The Romans employed crucifixion specifically as a means of intimidation. The public spectacle of crucified prisoners writhing in pain was an all too real advertisement of the fate awaiting anyone who dared resist or attempted to disrupt the finely tuned imperial machinery. That crucifixion *was* Jesus's fate speaks volumes about the way he must have comported himself during his earthly ministry. His was obviously a ministry of resistance, pure and simple. His ministry was a jihad.

Of course, the gospel writers have tried to hide this fact. They all in one way or another try to absolve the Romans of responsibility for the death of Jesus, shifting this responsibility over to the Jewish leaders. In Matthew and Mark, for example, Pilate proclaims Jesus's innocence. Matthew even has the Jewish crowds utter the fateful words of the blood libel: "His blood be on us and on our children." Luke goes a step further and has Pilate send Jesus to Herod for a second opinion about his guilt. Herod agrees with Pilate that Jesus is innocent, but the crowds bully Pilate into killing him anyway. In John, the Jews improbably affirm the sovereign nature of Caesar's rule over them, rejecting the title King of the Jews for Jesus. Now clearly, the picture of Pilate being bullied by his subjects, or of Jews proclaiming the kingship of Caesar, are not plausible scenarios, considering everything else we know about the relationship between Roman officials and their Jewish subjects. So why do the gospel writers try to hide Roman responsibility for the death of Jesus?

The Gospels were all written during the last quarter of the first century—after, that is, the Roman destruction of the Jewish temple in 70 CE. This violent Roman reaction to Jewish resistance made it all too clear that any kind of resistance to Rome would not be tolerated. Open rebellion was effectively a death sentence. Followers of Jesus could not risk telling his story in such a way as to openly point a finger of blame at the empire. It became crucial to tell a subversive story in a much less subversive way so as not to elicit Roman suspicions about the true aims of the Jesus movement. Moreover, the Roman destruction of the temple effectively eliminated priestly Judaism, leaving the Jewish followers of Jesus and the Pharisees as the only viable forms of Judaism in the latter stages of the first century. These two groups were locked in a struggle over the future of Judaism, and in this struggle it became convenient for the Jesus movement to point the finger of blame for the death of Jesus at their Pharisaic rivals. Roman officials would likely just yawn at what appeared to them as nothing more than an intra-Jewish struggle.

The necessity of obscuring the politically subversive nature of Jesus may help account for one of the best-known but most misunderstood of his sayings. Those who would deny the anti-Roman flavor of Jesus's actions often point to his famous saying "Render unto Caesar the things that are Caesar's and to God the things that are God's" to support their view of an apolitical Jesus, interpreting this statement as a sort of first-century affirmation of the separation of church and state. Jesus clearly wants to keep religion (the things of God) and politics (the things of Caesar) separate. But nothing could be further from the truth. Let's consider this popular vignette in more detail.

We are told that a group of Pharisees and Herodians approached Jesus with the very intention of entrapping him. They inquire, "Is it lawful to pay taxes to Caesar?" If Jesus replies in the affirmative, he will lose authority with his Jewish followers, who felt crushed by the burden of the Roman taxation system. But if he says no, Roman officials will come down hard on him, accusing him of fomenting rebellion. So what does Jesus do? He asks someone in the crowd to produce a coin. In response, someone pulls out a Roman *denarius* prompting Jesus to inquire, "Whose image is on this coin?" The crowd responds correctly, "Caesar's." In response, Jesus utters the famous saying, "Give to Caesar the things that are Caesar's and to God the things that are God's." Unfortunately, English translations have completely missed a crucial nuance in the original Greek text of this oft-repeated aphorism.

When Jesus's adversaries insincerely inquire into the legality of paying taxes to Caesar, they are not asking about taxes in the way we think about taxes today: as money paid to the government in return for public services. Imperial subjects were not afforded the kinds of municipal services in return for tax payments that we take for granted today. What Jesus's adversaries *are* asking about is whether it is allowable under Jewish law to participate in the imperial tribute system, a system that required its participants to acknowledge the divinity of the emperor. They are really asking, "Is it lawful to give tribute to Caesar?" The word here translated "give" is the Greek word *didomi*, which means "to give freely, as a gift." So Jesus's adversaries want to see if they can force Jesus to either affirm or deny willful participation in the tribute system: an affirmation would truly anger his Jewish followers, and a denial would provoke Roman wrath. It is one thing to be *forced* to participate, quite another to do so willingly. Jesus, for his part, fails to take the bait. Responding to the appearance of the coin bearing Caesar's image, Jesus says, "Return [*apodidomi*, in Greek] to Caesar what is his and to God what is God's." Jesus employs a different word, one that carries the force of rejection of the Roman tribute system along with the restoration to God of what rightfully belongs to God. But what belongs to God? Everything! This is the whole point of Jesus's proclamation of the coming of God's reign. So Jesus's famous statement *is* a rejection of Roman claims to sovereignty put into the form of an aphorism that veils its subversive meaning. And the veiling worked. Christians have misinterpreted this saying for two thousand years!

If Jesus was merely a spiritual teacher little interested in addressing the oppressive ways of the Roman Empire, Roman reaction to him (crucifixion) would be hard to square with their reaction to another first-century figure also named Jesus. Josephus tells the story of a man named Jesus son of Ananias whom he refers to as a rude peasant who lived sometime in the 60s CE. At a time when Josephus claims Jerusalem was enjoying profound peace and prosperity (for a few, no doubt!), Jesus son of Ananias appeared in Jerusalem hurling threats and predictions of destruction against the temple:

> A voice from the east, a voice from the west, a voice from the four winds; a voice against Jerusalem and the sanctuary, a voice against the bridegroom and the bride, a voice against all people.[13]

He repeated this cry daily until some of the leading citizens arrested and chastised him but to no avail. Jesus just went right on with his wailing against the city until magistrates, believing he might be under some sort of demonic spell, brought him to the Roman governor. The Roman officials whipped him brutally until his flesh was flayed to the bone, but Jesus endured the punishment stoically, failing to stop his cry of dereliction. Finally, the Roman governor proclaimed him to be a maniac and released him. Jesus son of Ananias continued his campaign for another seven years until he was finally killed in the Roman destruction of the city in 70 CE.

Why was Jesus son of Ananias released while Jesus of Nazareth was crucified? Clearly, Jesus son of Ananias was considered a crazy person and no real threat to imperial stability. He apparently had no followers but was just a lone voice of prophetic critique. But Jesus of Nazareth had a following. Crowds gathered to hail him using a messianic title (Son of David), imploring him to save them with the pleading cry of hosanna. The Romans were not stupid. They could see what was happening. Jesus of Nazareth was a threat to imperial stability. His ministry could not be tolerated. He had to be crucified. The Roman reaction to Jesus of Nazareth, on the one hand, and the Roman reaction to Jesus son of Ananias, on the other, show that Jesus of Nazareth must have been considered a dangerous leader of a prophetic, anti-Roman movement.

---

13. Thackeray, trans., Josephus, *Jewish War* 6.301.

It is really quite amazing that more Christians have not recognized the highly prophetic nature of Jesus's ministry. The evidence is all over the Gospels, and it is not always as subtle as some of what we have already seen. Luke's version of Jesus's famous beatitudes (what televangelist Robert Schuller once absurdly referred to as "The Be Happy Attitudes") begins this way:

> Blessed are you who are poor,
>> for yours is the kingdom of God.
> Blessed are you who are hungry now,
>> for you will be filled. (Luke 6:20–21)

This is followed up a few verses later with its direct antithesis:

> But woe to you who are rich,
>> for you have received your consolation.
> Woe to you who are full now,
>> for you will be hungry. (Luke 6:24–25)

A Jesus who condemns the rich and powerful to hunger does not sound like the sugary-sweet Jesus of Sunday School who loves and cares for everyone. This is a prophetic Jesus calling the powerful to account while envisioning a revolutionary reversal of the socioeconomic system of Roman Palestine.[14]

And how have we missed the parable of the rich man and Lazarus? Here the poor man covered with sores who grovels at the gates of a rich man is given a name, an identity. But the rich man? Well, he is just a rich man, a generic figure of economic exploitation. When the rich man and Lazarus both die, Lazarus ends up in heaven while the rich man is consigned to the realm of eternal torment. The rich man cries out for mercy, outrageously still trying to treat Lazarus like a servant, requesting Lazarus to dip his own finger in the cool water and touch the rich man's agonizingly parched lips—but to no avail. The yawning chasm opened up between Lazarus and the rich man in eternity is unbridgeable. There is no possibility for mercy for the rich man. He had his rewards in his earthly life. Now he is consigned to eternal damnation. Again, where is the warm, fuzzy Jesus of pietistic tradition here? This is a harsh prophetic warning for a Roman elite bent on brutally oppressing the nameless mass of Jewish peasants. Jesus's message is deadly serious and not for the faint of heart. Jesus was leading a jihad.

---

14. See Hanson, "How Honorable! How Shameful!"

JESUS AND JIHAD

If Jesus *was* a prophetic figure waging a jihad against the Roman Empire, how did this view of Jesus virtually disappear from Christian tradition until now? Why was the message of Jesus spiritualized by his followers? This is a complicated story beyond my ability to narrate in detail here. But we must realize that Roman imperial power itself played a significant role in this transformation. Following the brutal Roman destruction of the Jewish resistance movement in 70 CE, it would have become obvious to Jesus's followers that resistance to Roman power was futile. To resist was a death sentence. Jesus's followers, therefore, began to reinterpret Jesus in such a way as not to raise imperial suspicions. This movement toward reinterpretation is evident in the Gospel of John.

Unlike Matthew, Mark, and Luke, John does not portray Jesus as proclaiming the coming of the kingdom of God. In fact, Jesus does not even tell a single parable in the Gospel of John. Instead in John, *Jesus* becomes the central message of the gospel. Rather than pointing beyond himself to the coming of something greater than himself—God's kingdom—Jesus in John makes himself the focus of the message with a series of "I am" sayings—"I am the light of the world," "I am the resurrection and the life," "I am the good shepherd," and so forth. Resistance to Rome is subordinated to belief in Jesus and the promise of eternal life for those who believe. Jesus is now the "lamb of God who takes away the sins of the world"—an atoning sacrifice. Jesus's crucifixion is now part of God's plan of salvation for the world; it is not simply a Roman action of execution of a supposed treasonous criminal. John's Jesus has fully acquiesced to the realities of Roman imperial power. One can now be a follower of Jesus without needing to be involved in anti-Roman activity.

This theme is pulled through the later writings of the New Testament as well. In the letters of Ephesians and Colossians, letters written in the latter stages of the first century, we find strong evidence that the followers of Jesus were accommodating to the Roman imperial system. The so-called Household Codes in Ephesians chapters 5 and 6 (also in Colossians 3 and 4) exhort children to obey their parents, wives to be subject to their husbands, and slaves to obey their masters. This hierarchical social order mirrors the hierarchical order of the Roman social system and is a far cry from the vision articulated by the Apostle Paul in Gal 3:28: "There is no longer Jew or Greek, there is no longer slave or free, there is no longer male and female; for all of you are one in Christ Jesus." Paul's radically egalitarian vision is a direct affront to the stability of the Roman hierarchical system that helped to maintain the social order the Roman elite so highly prized. But the Household Codes in Ephesians and Colossians show how the Jesus movement began to accommodate to rather than resist the imperial order. By the early second century, when the book of 1 Timothy was written, the emerging imperial church had become fully institutionalized. It was now hierarchical and patriarchal, complete with elders, bishops, deacons, and the exhortation to "let a woman learn in silence with full submission. I permit no woman to teach or to have authority over a man; she is to keep silent" (1 Tim 2:11). The imperial, patriarchal church had been born—an imperial church that would by the fourth century under the Emperor Constantine become the purveyor of official religion in the empire—and the rest as they say is history.

Perhaps there is no more outrageous example of imperial accommodation in the New Testament than in the letter of 1 Peter. There we find this disturbing advice:

> For the Lord's sake accept the authority of every human institution, whether of the emperor as supreme, or of governors, as sent by him to punish those who do wrong and to praise those who do right. For it is God's will that by doing right you should silence the ignorance of the foolish . . . Honor everyone. Love the family of believers. Fear God. Honor the emperor.
>
> Slaves, accept the authority of your masters with all deference, not only those who are kind and gentle but also those who are harsh. For it is a credit to you if, being aware of God, you endure pain while suffering unjustly. If you endure when you are beaten for doing wrong, what credit is that? But if you endure when you do right and suffer for it, you have God's approval. For to this you have been called, because Christ also suffered for you, leaving you an example, so that you should follow in his steps. (1 Pet 2: 13–21)

In other words, honor the emperor that brutally oppresses and exploits you. Humbly accept the system of slavery, and be happy when your slave master beats the living daylights out of you because God will credit to you your endurance just as Jesus was privileged to suffer. This represents a complete and total theological justification for the worst effects of imperial oppression. The anti-Roman Jesus movement has been completely domesticated and has surrendered its prophetic heart. Imperial power itself defeated the prophetic heart of Christianity.

But times change, and the prophetic spirit of Jesus did not disappear entirely. There has always been a struggle within Christianity between the forces of an apolitical piety and a prophetic, political movement. Most recently, the twentieth century produced three outstanding examples of prophetic Christianity in action: the Social Gospel movement, liberation theology, and black theology. Each richly deserves a brief comment, for these three movements can provide the paradigm for the recovery of a jihad-oriented, prophetic Christianity in the twenty-first century.

The Social Gospel

In 1907 Walter Rauschenbusch, a Baptist pastor who led a church in the Hell's Kitchen neighborhood of Harlem, published his classic defense of a prophetic Christianity: *Christianity and the Social Crisis*. At a time when American society was marked by high levels of wealth inequality, Rauschenbusch recognized that a Jesus whose message had nothing to say to the material poverty of his poor, struggling parishioners was an irrelevant Jesus. His parishioners did not need to hear about a Jesus who would save them from their sins and take them to heaven when they died. They needed to hear about a Jesus who stands prophetically against economic exploitation and political corruption. The publication of *Christianity and the Social Crisis* spawned what came to be known as the Social Gospel movement, a movement that gained many adherents during the first half of the twentieth century. I will engage Rauschenbusch's work in a bit more detail in the next chapter where I will argue that Rauschenbusch stands as a premier example of a Christian waging a responsible jihad.

For now, we must remember that the early twentieth-century period that formed the backdrop for Rauschenbusch's life witnessed an America dominated by the fabulously wealthy capitalist magnates like the Carnegies, Vanderbilts, and Rockefellers. But while a few Americans were living high off the hog, many, including Rauschenbusch's parishioners, were struggling with subsistence wages, poor working conditions, and little access to basic health care. Sound familiar? Did Jesus have any relevance in the face of issues like economic injustice? Rauschenbusch certainly thought so, but far too many Christians today don't. Rauschenbusch's Jesus motivated his followers past and present to a life of jihad against the forces of injustice. Jesus for him was a purely prophetic figure. Of course, economic injustice is not unique to America. It plagued societies in Latin America in the middle of the twentieth century and spawned the movement known as liberation theology.

Liberation Theology

In the Latin America of the mid-twentieth century, the Roman Catholic Church came to be viewed by many people as a tacit supporter of the unjust status quo. In reaction the Peruvian scholar Gustavo Gutiérrez published *A Theology of Liberation* in 1973 and the liberation theology movement was born. Gutiérrez argued that people could no longer look to the Roman Catholic Church to address the miseries of their material conditions. They needed instead to take hold of the reins and view themselves as masters of their own destiny. They could no longer rely on the Church, but needed to participate in their own liberation—defined here not as liberation of the soul from sin but rather as liberation from the deleterious effects of unjust social and economic relationships.[15]

As Rauschenbusch does, so Gutiérrez also highlights how Christianity had come to revolve completely around the institution of the church. The church had become the center of all theological reflection in what Gutiérrez calls "an ecclesiocentric perspective that centered more and more on the life and reflection of the Church—and continues to do so up to the present time."[16] Liberation theology countered this "ecclesiocentric perspective" by "uncentering" the church and moving the ground of theological reflection out into the real world of people's everyday lives and their struggle for existence. The gospel message had to transcend the boundaries of the church, and instead animate ordinary citizens to participate in a revolutionary political struggle against the entrenched powers of an unjust political and economic system. That is, liberation theology exhorted its followers to engage in a jihad. All this was based on a profoundly political understanding of the message of Jesus. Not surprisingly, when the struggle for civil rights erupted in America in the 1950s and 1960s, liberation theology became the paradigm for the development of a black theology movement.

15. Gutiérrez, *Theology of Liberation*, 68.
16. Ibid., 257.

Black Theology

While the people of Latin America struggled with the effects of economic injustice, black people in the United States began to mobilize against racial injustice. (Yes, Rosa Parks was a mujahid!) The civil rights movement was the soil out of which grew a specifically black theology movement. While many important thinkers helped shape black theology, one of the outstanding spokespersons has been James Cone. With the publication in 1975 of his bold liberatory reading of Christian tradition, *God of the Oppressed*, Cone unravels centuries of Christian theology by flatly declaring, "Any interpretation of the gospel in any historical period that fails to see Jesus as the Liberator of the oppressed is heretical."[17] Cone believed that Scripture had allowed slaves to affirm a view of God that differed in dramatic ways from the view of the slave masters, who presented a Jesus designed to make slaves docile and obedient.[18] (Recall the passage from 1 Peter above!)

For Cone, and for black theology in general, the gospel preached by Jesus can never be identified with the established power of the state. This is the error made by early Christians in allowing Christianity to become the official religion of the Roman Empire. Jesus was committed to revolutionary action against injustice, slavery, and oppression. Liberation is not about salvation from sin; "it is the sociohistorical movement of a people from oppression to freedom."[19] In short, the struggle for liberation is jihad.

Given the obvious political nature of the biblical text, Cone wonders how biblical scholars have missed this and instead have supported the traditional portrait of Jesus as an apolitical religious figure. The answer is not hard to come by. Cone believes white theologians' views of Jesus are influenced by a prior commitment to the social structures of oppression. They are blind to the radical political nature of Jesus's work because "their vision is committed to the very structures that Jesus despised."[20] This is an important insight. Christianity has been, through most of its history, an imperial religion, and therefore its texts and traditions have naturally been interpreted in ways that support the imperial status quo. Prophetic Christianity has failed to dominate throughout history precisely because Christianity has been co-opted by the forces of injustice and oppression.

17. Cone, *God of the Oppressed*, 37.
18. Ibid., 31.
19. Ibid., 152.
20. Ibid., 223.

It has been those in marginal communities—those who struggle with the negative effects of the imperial beast—who can see Jesus for who he really was—a prophetic figure waging jihad.

We might note here that in the contemporary world, ever greater numbers of people are falling into the category of the marginalized. They are no longer a minority (if they ever were). The vast majority of the world's people are straining under the weight of a corporate-dominated global capitalist system that operates on exploitation of people, resources, and the entire ecological system of the planet. If Jesus is not relevant to the material lives of these people then Jesus is not relevant—period! It is time for a responsible jihad. But waging such a jihad will require that we transcend superficial religious-identity labels and engage a depth of spirituality that the secularization of modern life is rendering increasingly untenable. How might Christians and Muslims overcome these obstacles and begin to wage a responsible jihad? In the final two chapters I will try to lay out a vision that seeks to answer this important and profound question.

5

Waging a Responsible Jihad

*Declare your jihad on thirteen enemies you cannot see—egoism,
arrogance, conceit, selfishness, greed, lust, intolerance, anger, lying,
cheating, gossiping, and slandering. If you can master and destroy
them, then you will be ready to fight the enemy you can see.*

—AL-GHAZALI

The great medieval Islamic scholar al-Ghazali has perfectly articulated
what it will take to wage a contemporary jihad against the myriad systems of injustice and oppression plaguing the modern world. The world
today is in dire need of a jihad, but this cannot be just any jihad. We need
a jihad that, unlike the jihads waged by Islamic terrorists, refuses to perpetuate the kinds of violence and injustice jihad is designed to resist. In
short, we need a responsible jihad. Following the wise words of al-Ghazali,
then, a responsible jihad will first require defeating the human penchant
for egoism, conceit, and selfishness that stems from superficial religiosity
and the concomitant loss of deep spiritual connection. Specifically, both
Christians and Muslims will need to transcend the narrowly conceived
religious-identity labels they cling to so tightly in our secular age. This may
prove to be a Herculean task, for we have an almost pathological aversion
to anything that tries to turn our attention away from the superficial, the

frivolous, the mundane (as Facebook and Twitter attest). But I do not believe it is impossible. Let me try to chart a course for how we might develop an appreciation for the value of transcending superficial religious-identity labels in order that we may open to the kind of deep spiritual connection that organically leads to the kind of responsible jihad the world craves and that we are called to supply.

THE PROBLEM OF RELIGIOUS-IDENTITY OBSESSION

Why must we transcend narrowly conceived religious-identity labels to be able to wage a responsible jihad? What is wrong with asserting an exclusive identity as a Muslim or Christian? The relationship between exclusive religious-identity claims and the ability to engage in the struggle for a more just world may not be obvious, but understanding the relationship is crucial for coming to terms with perhaps the chief obstacle to the reclaiming of a prophetic heart. Let me explain this critical connection.

We live in a world where an increasing number of people derive their entire sense of personal identity from membership in a particular religious community conceived as an entity mutually exclusive to all other religious communities. A person might say, "I am a Christian," and by doing so mean to indicate that he or she is by definition not a Jew, Muslim, Buddhist, or atheist. For this person, being identified as Christian is more important than claiming identity based on ethnicity, national origin, or just simply asserting one's identity as a member of the human family. For this person, Christian identity is not first and foremost about living a life in accordance with the teachings and practices of Jesus Christ; it is rather about claiming an exclusive religious identity and participating in a community of like-minded individuals who also make identical exclusive religious-identity claims. As I mentioned earlier, we might call this Religious-Identity Obsession Syndrome.

Perhaps the easiest place to see a Christian version of the syndrome at work is in American politics. Theoretically, people of any or no religious background are eligible to hold elected office in the United States. This is guaranteed by the U.S. Constitution, which forbids a religious test for public office. So why has every president been at least nominally Christian (and almost all Protestant)? Why did President Obama's opponents try to demonize him as a Muslim in order to delegitimize his candidacy in the 2008 presidential campaign? Why was there concern expressed over Mitt

Romney's Mormon identity in the 2012 campaign? Why does it strain credulity to even raise the specter of a Muslim, Hindu, or unabashedly atheist candidate being elected president of the United States? Because there clearly *is* a tacit religious test for public office even if there is not an official one. Many Christians, who remain the dominant religious group in an increasingly religiously diverse nation, want their president to be a Christian just like them. But what are they really saying?

Why shouldn't a presidential candidate's political philosophy, personal integrity, or positions on policy issues be the most important characteristics for evaluating fitness for public office? Aren't these more important—and more determinative—for how a candidate will function as president? Can't a Buddhist share one's political philosophy? Can't a Muslim hold policy positions that resonate with one's own? Can't an atheist be a person of impeccable personal and moral integrity? Of course. But don't try to tell this to your average Christian voter. The president must be a Christian just like them, a president who ends every public address with the perfunctory "God bless the United States of America." This is Religious-Identity Obsession Syndrome at work.

Another manifestation of Religious-Identity Obsession Syndrome among Christians is the phenomenon of contemporary Christian music, especially Christian rock and Christian heavy metal. It used to be that the term "Christian music" meant hymns sung in church or anthems performed by choirs. But now virtually every genre of "secular" music has its Christian counterpart. As long as we can put the adjective *Christian* in front of hip hop, for example, it is okay for Christians to listen to. The idea of course is that Christians would be corrupted by listening to "secular" music. I don't know. I grew up listening to The Beatles, Pink Floyd, the Who, Led Zeppelin, and many other (non-Christian) rock bands, and I turned out okay (though the Christians I am talking about here would certainly disagree given that I have written a book titled *Jesus and Jihad*!). Christians today wear their religion as an identity label in all kinds of ways: through those ubiquitous WWJD bracelets, through tattoos of Bible verses, through T-shirts adorned with pious platitudes of the most superficial kind. Being a Christian simply means identifying oneself as such and then announcing it clearly and loudly to everyone else. What is missing from so many modern Western Christians is any evidence of a deep and mature spirituality. And this is a major reason why the Christian prophetic voice is quickly waning. It should not escape our attention that one of the least prophetic forms of

Christianity—a specific group of white-supremacist Christians—actually refers to itself as the Christian *Identity* Movement! This is a particularly egregious example, but it illustrates the problematic connection between religious-identity obsession and support for injustice. Shorn of any connection to deep spiritual resources, identity-obsessed Christians become participants in the kinds of systems of injustice that a responsible jihad would resist.

Unfortunately, Muslims have not escaped Religious-Identity Obsession Syndrome either. Being a Muslim is fast becoming defined simply as adhering to the Five Pillars as a set of rituals (without a strong sense of what those rituals mean or why they exist) as well as identifying with other like-minded Muslims who view Islam as superior to all other religions. For some Muslim men, sporting a beard in imitation of the Prophet Muhammad is as important to their sense of Muslim identity as anything they actually do to make the world a better place. I noted earlier the apologetic exploits of Dr. Zakir Naik. He is just one among many such figures that can be found all over the Internet extolling the virtues of Islam and proving (with facile and tendentious arguments) its inherent superiority over all other religions. The tremendous energy spent by Muslim teachers on these superficial and utterly meaningless apologetic exploits is strong testimony to the tragic loss of deep spiritual connection suffered by too many of the world's 1.5 billion Muslims.

The danger here is that when Islam devolves to the level of a superficial religious-identity label, jihad can easily be reframed as a movement whose primary goal becomes the growth of a confessionally specific Muslim community. Rather than understanding jihad as a movement of social transformation toward greater levels of justice for all people, identity-obsessed Muslims are more likely to view jihad as the struggle to bring the world under the umbrella of a confessionally specific Islam in which all people would practice the Five Pillars and adopt any number of specifically Muslim characteristics having to do with clothing, cuisine, language, and so forth. I have no doubt that Muslim apologists like Zakir Naik view their apologetic campaign as a jihad. If Islam is found to be superior to all other religions, then it stands to reason that all people should adopt a Muslim identity, and it is incumbent upon Muslims to try and bring this about. The fear expressed by Americans that jihad is a method for converting the whole world to Islam may not be entirely unfounded even if the immediacy of the threat is greatly exaggerated.

More disturbing, perhaps, than the effect of Religious-Identity Obsession Syndrome on contemporary religious groups in Western countries is the effect of the syndrome on the way so-called jihads are actually carried out around the world. Palestinian suicide bombers, al-Qaeda and ISIS operatives, anti-Shi'ite militants, and other Muslim groups who opt for terrorism and violence unabashedly subsume their activities under the banner of jihad. But can any activity be considered a form of jihad when it results in the gratuitous deaths of innocent people, especially children? Absolutely not! A Muslim like Emir Abd el-Kader would shudder at how the concept jihad is being corrupted by identity-obsessed Muslims today. But where Islam becomes little more than an identity label, the loss of connection to deep spiritual resources very easily leads to a loss of empathy for the suffering of others and therefore to a reliance on the indiscriminate use of violence divorced from any clear strategic imperative.

This transformation of Christianity and Islam into personal-identity labels points to a loss of deep spiritual connection within both traditions caused by the rampant spread of secularism. Any jihad waged from this superficial mindset is bound to go awry. A responsible jihad must be rooted in a deep and mature spirituality in order to maintain its focus on the struggle for justice for all people (no matter what religious label they wear) and in order to maintain an uncompromising belief in the dignity of all forms of life. A responsible jihad cannot be waged without Muslims and Christians first being willing to confront their superficial religious-identity obsessions and discard them. Doing so will not be easy for deep psychological reasons I will explore later in this chapter. But I am convinced it will not be impossible either. A place to begin is to recognize that religious-identity obsession did not characterize the early movements that came to be known as Christianity and Islam. Neither Jesus nor Muhammad appears to have been afflicted by Religious-Identity Obsession Syndrome. Let's consider the evidence for this striking observation, beginning with Islam.

TRANSCENDING RELIGIOUS-IDENTITY OBSESSION IN ISLAM

I already noted in chapter 2 how the respected historian of Islam, Fred M. Donner, provides compelling evidence for a view of Islamic origins somewhat different from the traditional view perpetuated by Muslims. Recall that Donner labels the early Islamic movement a Believers' movement based on the repeated phrase in the Qur'an "O, you who believe," which occurs more than 1000 times. He characterizes this Believers' movement as a monotheistic reform movement that likely included Jews, Christians, Zoroastrians, and former pagan Arabs who unified around the idea of submission to one God. Let's consider Donner's evidence for this potentially revolutionary reconstruction of Islamic origins in greater detail to really grasp its implications for today's identity-obsessed Muslims.

As a historian, Donner prioritizes documentary evidence in his reconstruction of the self-understanding of this early Believers' movement. Though his relabeling of the Muslim movement as a Believers' movement is based primarily on evidence from the Qur'an, the qur'anic evidence is strongly supported by early inscriptions, coins, and papyri, in which Muhammad's early successors, known traditionally as caliphs (*caliph* is Arabic for "successor") actually appear to have referred to themselves with the title, *amir al-mu'minin* ("Commander of the Believers").[1] The traditional title caliph does not appear in the documentary record until well past the time of Muhammad and his earliest "successors." This is an important point. It shows that the self-understanding of the earliest movement was different from how the later tradition would come to view it. Muhammad and his followers saw themselves as Believers, not Muslims. While this evidence is highly suggestive, it pales in comparison to the significance of what comes next.

At the heart of modern Muslim identity is the first of Islam's Five Pillars, the Shahadah, or confession of faith. Sincerely repeating this confession "There is no god but the God, and Muhammad is the Messenger of the God" is said to render a person a Muslim. Of course, this confession is specific to Muslims; Christians and Jews could likely affirm the first half of the Shahadah (There is no god but the God), but the second half attesting to Muhammad's unique status as Messenger renders the Shahadah a specifically Islamic statement of belief. But this again is where Donner's work is so suggestive. According to Donner, all early attestations of the Shahadah found on coins, inscriptions, and papyri contain only the generic confession of God's oneness. ("There is no god but the God.") The confessionally specific second half of the Shahadah so integral to modern Muslim identity is missing in all this early documentary evidence. The full Shahadah does not appear in the documentary record, according to Donner, until after

---

1. Donner, *Muhammad and the Believers*, 99.

685 CE—more than fifty years after Muhammad's death.[2] This is powerful evidence for the view that Islam did not begin as a new religious identity distinct from Judaism, Christianity, Zoroastrianism, or other religions. It was a movement of social transformation, and its members were not obsessed with religious identity labels. The movement included people from a variety of so-called religious backgrounds. One cannot overstate the importance of this documentary evidence showing the originality of a shortened, nonconfessionally specific, form of the Shahadah. But even more fascinating, this documentary evidence finds expression even in later Muslim literary sources, where we might expect it to have been erased.

For example, recall the tradition (discussed in chapter three) about Muhammad's upbraiding the young man named Usamah who had killed an adversary in battle despite the victim's having pronounced the Shahadah at the point of Usamah's sword. The Shahadah appears in this story repeatedly in the same truncated form found in early coins and inscriptions. When Usamah catches up to the man and wounds him, we are told the man shouted out *la ilaha illa Llah* (There is no god but the God). When Usamah then repeats this story to his fellow combatants, he again recites the Shahadah in the short form. Later when he comes before Muhammad and tells the story, Muhammad inquires, "Did you, O Usamah, slay him when he had said *la ilaha illa Llah*?" Convicted by Muhammad's question, Usamah replies, "Never again will I slay any man who says *la ilaha illa Llah*."[3] The absence here of the second half of the familiar Shahadah formula—*wamuhammadun rasulu Llah* (and Muhammad is the messenger of the God)—even on the lips of Muhammad in a traditional Muslim literary source—is strong evidence for the idea that the full Shahadah so central to Muslim identity today was a secondary development.

This will be an idea difficult for many modern Muslims to accept; the full Shahadah is so central a part of their religious lives. How could it not be original? I presented this material at a conference recently and was predictably taken to task by some Muslims in the audience for ignoring the fact that the full Shahadah occurs in the Qur'an, and, I was firmly reminded, the Qur'an is certainly more authoritative than early coins and inscriptions! Let me address this critique because it is at most only half right.

The full Shahadah as it is known today does not appear in its entirety anywhere in the Qur'an. The two parts of the Shahadah do appear, but in

2. Ibid, 112.

3. See Lings, *Muhammad*, 274.

separate places. The first part—*la ilaha illa Llah*—is found twice (37:35; 47:19). The second part—*wamuhammadun rasulu Llah*—occurs only once (48:29). So the individual phrases that will later compose the Shahadah do find expression in the Qur'an, but, as Andrew Rippen argues, the Shahadah does not appear in the Qur'an as a confessional formula, "nor is there any indication of the ritual act which later Islam made of it."[4] Surah 48:29 affirms the status of Muhammad as the messenger of God as a statement of fact but gives no indication that Muslims are called upon to repeat this statement as a ritual act. In a similar way, Christians can find scattered in various parts of the New Testament the ideas expressed in the Apostles' Creed, but the Apostles' Creed as a confessional formula does not appear anywhere in the New Testament and clearly arose much later. It is difficult to avoid the conclusion that the Shahadah arose as simply an affirmation of the oneness of God; the confessionally specific second part arose only secondarily, as this early, nonconfessional Believers' movement morphed into the more confessionally specific religious tradition of Islam.

But this is not all. Fred Donner argues further that the words *islam* and *muslim* in the Qur'an do not carry the sense of confessional distinctness we have come to associate with the English terms "Islam" and "Muslim."[5] The written Arabic language, unlike written English, does not feature both uppercase and lowercase letters. So when the Qur'an uses the Arabic word *muslim*, for example, we have to ask whether it is meant in a generic sense to refer to "one who submits" or in a confessionally specific sense to refer to someone who recites the Qur'an in Arabic, prays five times a day facing Mecca, and fasts during Ramadan. The context of the Qur'an would seem to indicate the more general meaning, as the following examples illustrate.

Surah 10:90 presents the story familiar from the biblical book of Exodus of Pharaoh pursuing the liberated Israelite slaves through the Red Sea (actually Sea of Reeds). In the Qur'an Pharaoh cries out, "I have come to believe that there is no deity save Him in whom the children of Israel believe, and I am of those who surrender themselves [*muslim*] unto Him." This use of the word *muslim* can clearly not be meant to denote the confessionally specific identity Muslim since Pharaoh lived long before any identifiable Muslim movement existed. Pharaoh is merely pointing out here an attitude toward life that he is adopting—that of submission to the God of Israel. Similarly, Surah 12:101 portrays Joseph, the son of Jacob known so

4. Rippen, "Witness to Faith," 488.
5. Donner, *Muhammad and the Believers*, 71.

well from the famous story in Genesis as beseeching God to "let me die as one who has surrendered himself (*muslim*) unto Thee, and make me one with the righteous!" Joseph, of course, was not a Muslim, but he certainly could be considered "one who submits" (a muslim). Surah 51:36 has Lot reporting to Abraham during the Sodom and Gomorrah episode that he has been able to find submitters (*muslims*) in only one house. Of course, Lot would be hard pressed to find confessionally specific Muslims running around more than two thousand years prior to the advent of a confessionally specific Muslim movement! By repeatedly referring to pre-Islamic figures using the Arabic term *muslim*, the Qur'an must intend for this word to be taken in its generic meaning, as simply referring to an attitude or orientation to life—that of submission.

As more evidence, the grammatical context of Surah 29:46 *requires* a generic meaning for *muslim*. The receivers of the revelation are instructed to say to the People of the Book (Jews and Christians):

> We believe in that which has been bestowed from on high upon us,
>   as well as that which has been bestowed upon you;
> for our God and your God is one and the same,
>   and it is unto him that we surrender ourselves (*muslim*)

It would make little grammatical sense to say "to him we are Muslims." The term *muslim* clearly has a verbal force here—"to him we surrender ourselves." Perhaps Surah 72:14 is the clincher. Here we read, "Yet it is true that among us are such as have surrendered themselves (*muslim*) to God—just as there are among us such as have abandoned themselves to wrongdoing." By placing *muslim* in opposition to "abandon themselves to wrongdoing," the Qur'an clearly means for *muslim* to refer to a generic action that could theoretically apply to anyone: the opposite of abandoning oneself to wrongdoing.

In light of these examples and the reality that the Arabic language makes no distinction (as written English does) between the capitalized word *Muslim* and the lowercased word *muslim*, it is virtually certain that the Qur'an only recognizes one meaning of the Arabic term *muslim*: the generic meaning. Said another way, there is no evidence that the receivers of the qur'anic revelation—those we would refer to as Muslims today—were ever addressed originally with any kind of religious-identity label at all in the Qur'an itself. Islam did not originate as a new religious identity, and its early adherents could not therefore have been afflicted with Religious-Identity Obsession Syndrome. Islam was rather a dynamic movement of social transformation. One *acted* as a muslim (one who submits); one did not merely ascribe to the identity label Muslim.

Eventually, by the eighth century, according to Donner, the Believers' movement would begin to transform into the more confessionally specific Islam that we know today, complete with the expanded version of the Shahadah attesting to Muhammad's role as the Messenger of God. The reasons for this transformation are complex and beyond our scope here, but this transformation likely also involved the development of the Five Pillars as the defining set of actions for what it means to be a part of this confessionally specific, Muslim community. Yet the seeds of the Five Pillars undoubtedly lie in the earlier Believers' movement, and it is crucial to understand them in this earlier context, for understanding the purpose of the pillars will be critical for any hope of enacting a responsible jihad.

Textbooks on Islam will generally describe the Five Pillars as a set of religious rituals that define what it means to be a Muslim. Such books generally go on to describe what the Five Pillars are and simply leave it at that. But the pillars are much more than religious rituals. For those not familiar with them, the Five Pillars consist of confessing the Shahadah, praying five times a day, giving *zakat* (frequently, but incorrectly, described as almsgiving), fasting during the month of Ramadan, and making pilgrimage to Mecca. Simply listing what the pillars entail is one thing. More important is to consider why the pillars exist as they do. What is the intention behind them? Recall the story I told in chapter two about how the Emir of the Islamic Organization of North America during Friday prayers at a large mosque in Silicon Valley exhorted his fellow Muslims to consider the nature of pillars. Pillars, of course, are never the whole of a building; they are merely its support structure. The Five Pillars of Islam are likewise not the whole of Islam; they are the support structures that make Islam (a life of submission) possible. But how do they do this?

If, as I am arguing, Islam did not originate as a new confessionally specific religious tradition but as a movement of social transformation toward greater levels of justice, then the pillars cannot function as pillars unless they are in some way serving to support this transformative movement and render it possible. So what is the connection between praying five times a day and social justice, or between paying *zakat* and social transformation? This connection is really not that hard to see.

Let's begin with the first pillar, confessing the Shahadah. In what appears to have been its original form—There is no god but the God—the

Shahadah is the confession of one's belief in a single, unified deity (Allah in Arabic). This is a confession of the central concept on which Islamic thought is built: the concept of *tawhid* (unity). The term *tawhid* refers, not only to the idea of the absolute unity of God, but also to two other ideas: first, to the idea of a unified humanity living in submission to this one God; and, second, to the idea of a unified and integrated sense of reality such that no clear distinction can be made between a sacred and a secular realm. All reality is integrated in such a way that, for example, what we term spiritual teachings are just as much economic teachings and vice versa. There can be no meaningful "separation of church and state" in Islam (partly because there is no church in Islam! *Church* is a specifically Christian term). The Shahadah functions as a pillar of social transformation by reminding the confessor that all the actions of life—not just private spiritual acts but political ones too—must be performed in reference to divine reality. Human reason and ego are not able to provide proper guidance.

The Shahadah, while important, will not be enough to bring about social transformation by itself, however. The human ego is stubborn. We don't like to arrange our affairs in reference to a higher power to which we owe our willing submission. We would much prefer to make the rules ourselves in ways consistent with our own interests. (This is the chief characteristic of secularism.) So the second pillar, praying five times a day, is designed to tame the ego and to fully ingrain the idea of submission into the life of the Muslim community. How is this done? In an Islamic society, five times a day a call to prayer issues from the mosque, which begins with the phrase *allahu akbar* ("God is greater than . . ."). Greater than what, you ask? The comparative phrase here is left incomplete—intentionally, I suspect. When the call to prayer goes out, it is calling all Muslims to the awareness that God is greater than whatever they happen to be doing the moment the call to prayer is heard. If you are at school, God is greater. If you are transacting a business deal, God is greater. If you are involved in an athletic event, God is greater.

In response to this call, Muslims are expected to cease their activity and perform a short ritual prayer that includes physical prostration to fully embody the act of submission. The message here is that submission to God takes precedence over all else, and that whatever you happen to be doing at the moment the call to prayer goes out must be done in reference to that call for submission. Imagine how our politics might be different if sessions of Congress were routinely interrupted by prayer and physical prostration!

Maybe our senators and representatives would see superficial partisan bickering as the silly, useless exercise it is. A Muslim woman once said to me, "It is hard to have your nose up in the air when five times a day it is pressed on the floor." What great wisdom! Daily prostration in response to a reminder of the all-embracing nature of God tames the human ego and allows the Muslim community to design political, economic, and social structures that are not based on the ego-driven desire to accumulate power and wealth at the expense of the poor and the marginalized. Muslim prayer is indelibly linked to the development of a just society.

This brings us to the third pillar, *zakat*. Traditionally translated as "almsgiving" in religious-studies textbooks, *zakat* is no such thing. Calling it almsgiving mistakenly implies that *zakat* is some sort of voluntary charity to help the less fortunate. Actually, *zakat* is an annual tax levied on a person's accumulated wealth, to be distributed by the state to those in need in order to guarantee a basic standard of living for everyone. *Zakat* is a form of wealth redistribution designed to prevent the accumulation of too much wealth in too few hands—a situation that invariably leads to corruption, exploitation, and injustice. Submission to God implies that spiritual development must be prioritized over material accumulation as the goal of life. So, preventing the hoarding of wealth is part of a program of spiritual purification. *Zakat* is not a form of voluntary charity. It is in fact the pillar of an economic system designed to eliminate the very need for charity in the first place. Islam is not a tradition of unfettered capitalist wealth accumulation. (I will have more to say about Islamic economics in the next chapter.)

The final two pillars—fasting and pilgrimage—are also important for emphasizing the unity of the Muslim community in its life of submission, but I will refrain from a detailed discussion of them here. The larger point should be clear. The Five Pillars are not some random religious rituals that just happened to develop and then came to define what it means to be a Muslim. The pillars have a logic to them. They are a critical component of the move to re-create society in reference to divine rather human authority. Simply performing the pillars does not make one a Muslim. The pillars are the critical support structures that make it possible to develop just and equitable human relationships. Islam is the sum total of all those relationships—individual and communal—that issue in the development of just and peaceful societies.

The evidence is clear. Islam did not originate as a completely new religion mutually exclusive from existing religions in the seventh century.

Though it certainly became more confessionally specific over time, it did not begin this way. Taking this evidence seriously should give pause to modern Muslims who view Islam primarily as a religious-identity label. Identity-obsessed Muslims may actually be acting contrary to the character of the prophet whom they so revere and seek to imitate. Truly imitating Muhammad might entail transcending a specifically Muslim identity label in order to simply live like a muslim, to truly live a life of submission to God. Authentically following Muhammad would lead to the abandonment of superficial apologetic debates, misguided attempts to find Muhammad in the Bible, and the tribal temptation for retribution and violence. Being muslim means being engaged in a jihad supported by pillars that tame human ego (where the obsession with identity lies) and foster the desire to bring about justice and peace for all people. What's important is that the resources necessary to help Muslims transcend their obsession with religious identity are found within the Islamic tradition itself; they are not a foreign imposition. They just need to be reclaimed. Christianity must also claim its transcendent resources.

TRANSCENDING RELIGIOUS-IDENTITY OBSESSION IN CHRISTIANITY

As is the case with Islam, there is no real evidence that the movement spawned by Jesus originated as a new confessionally specific religious movement. First, we have to state the obvious—but frequently ignored—truth that Jesus himself was not a Christian. Jesus was a representative of first-century Palestinian Judaism, and there is little evidence that Judaism itself represented a unique religious identity at the time of Jesus. Probably it is more accurate to think of Jesus as a member of Judean society in a geographical or historical sense or both, and not as a member of Judaism in a reified religious sense. Given that there is no word for religion in the language of either the Hebrew Bible or the New Testament, we have to accept the striking fact that Jesus lived in a religionless world. Where there is no religion there can by definition be no adherence to an exclusive religious identity. Jesus could not adhere to something that simply did not exist.

So what did it mean in the first century to be a follower of Jesus? I essentially answered this question in the previous chapter. The multiple lines of evidence laid out there point to an understanding of Jesus as a highly political figure standing prophetically against the injustices endured by the

Palestinian people at the hands of the Roman Empire. Calling Jesus a political figure, of course, does not mean that his movement of resistance was not theologically motivated. Far from it. Jesus's work was deeply rooted in his belief that the world should be ruled by divine sovereignty (the kingdom of God), and that such a world would lead to greater levels of justice than one ruled by human sovereignty, at least as practiced by Roman imperial officials. Participating in Jesus's mission clearly meant engaging in a prophetic attempt to speak truth to power and transform society. Being a disciple of Jesus was not about personal spirituality or individual salvation. The depoliticized reading of the nature of Jesus's mission that dominates in contemporary Western Christianity was a secondary move that developed, as we saw in the previous chapter, primarily because of the overwhelming power of the empire itself and its ability—and desire—to ruthlessly crush any and all pretense to resistance.

Recall the earlier discussion pointing out the stark contrast between the way Jesus is portrayed in the Synoptic Gospels (Matthew, Mark, and Luke) and the portrait that emerges from the later Gospel of John. In the Synoptics, the overarching message of Jesus's teaching is his proclamation of the coming of the kingdom of God, with all the subversive political implications such a proclamation entails. In John, Jesus never proclaims the coming of the kingdom. He rather makes a series of "I am" statements—"I am the light of the world," "I am the resurrection and the life," "I am the way, the truth, and the life"—in order to place the focus on himself and make belief in him the central thrust of the gospel message. The Synoptic Jesus never utters a single "I am" saying. He instead tells parables to illuminate the subversive characteristics of the kingdom. John's Jesus, not surprisingly, never tells a single parable.

The contrast between the Jesus of the Synoptic Gospels and the Jesus of John's gospel is so stark as to render these portrayals as almost mutually exclusive. The two portrayals cannot both be historically accurate (if either is). The most likely explanation is that by the late first century when John was written, the followers of Jesus recognized the futility of active rebellion against the empire. In light of the empire's brutal crackdown on the Jewish resistance and destruction of the temple in 70 CE, it was plain to all that active rebellion was a virtual death sentence. To survive as a movement, the followers of Jesus were forced to attenuate the prophetic spirit of the Synoptic (and, I would argue, more historically authentic) Jesus, and to spiritualize the gospel in a way that would sit more easily with the reality of Roman sovereignty. No more proclaiming the subversive message of the coming of the kingdom of God. Now the gospel message was transformed into being about belief in Jesus as a divine messenger, salvation from sin, and eternal life (John 3:16). John's Jesus accommodates to the brutal imperial force that the Synoptic Jesus actively resists. So Christians have to make a choice. Which Jesus should they follow? What does it really mean to be a Christian?

This movement of accommodation to the empire continued on into the second and third centuries until by the fourth, Christianity became an imperial church under the rule of the Emperor Constantine. The imperialization of the church ensured that the spiritualized Jesus of John's gospel would become dominant within Christian theology, the political Jesus of the Synoptics being subordinated to this spiritualized portrayal and effectively ignored. (There is a reason why the famous evangelist Billy Graham gave out copies of John's gospel to the throngs of people who attended his crusades, but never the Synoptic Gospels). Belief in Jesus as Son of God and Savior becomes the hallmark of a uniquely Christian identity clearly distinct from Judaism, Islam, Buddhism, or other religions. Christianity became a personal-identity marker. But I don't believe this understanding is consistent with who Jesus really was. Can Christians give up their obsession with a religious identity based on a personal savior in order to encounter a prophetic Jesus calling them to political resistance and social transformation? This will not be easy, but neither is it impossible.

Some years ago, I was attending a chapel service at Luther College during Lent. The preacher that day was my religion department colleague who taught courses in Lutheran theology. She began her message by reflecting on the long-standing Christian tradition of giving something up during the period of Lent (like eating meat on Fridays). She then grappled with the question of what she was prepared to give up for Lent that particular year. After much thought, she concluded that she would give up the doctrine of the atonement! This was a bold (and amusing) message for a Lutheran theologian to deliver in a chapel service at a Lutheran college, but it is one necessary to hear. We saw in chapter 3 how the whole atonement system of temple sacrifice was part of the Roman imperial economy. Atonement theology, whereby sacrifices had to be made to ward off the wrath of an angry God, was simply a strategy to encourage the population to participate in their own exploitation. Jesus rightly rejected this system, and Christians should as well. More recently I was in an adult Sunday school class at the

Methodist church where I worship. The question was raised of how many people really believe that God sent Jesus to die for their sins. I was stunned, but gladdened, to observe that not a single hand went up. Atonement theology may finally be on its way out. Good riddance!

To truly be a follower of Jesus is to assume the prophetic mantle, to put aside all obsession with Christian identity, and to engage in the struggle to transform society on behalf of all suffering people. Jesus did not found a religion. He founded a prophetic movement. There is a big difference. There is no reason for modern Christians not to re-engage with this prophetic Jesus and put concern with religious identity aside. Identity-obsessed Christianity, just like identity-obsessed Islam, represents a failure of the prophetic spirit and a corruption of the character of those traditions' central figures.

There are thus all kinds of reasons for Muslims and Christians to give up viewing their respective traditions as superficial religious-identity labels. Confessionally specific Islam and confessionally specific Christianity are both secondary developments. Put more simply, Muhammad was not a Muslim (with a capital *M*). Heck, he didn't even pronounce the full Shahadah! Likewise, Jesus was not a Christian in any sense of what that religious label has come to mean today. It does not appear that he even believed in his own death as an atoning sacrifice for sin! Jesus and Muhammad both developed movements based around calling people to a new attitude and orientation to life, an attitude that would resist the drive for exploitative power and lead to greater levels of justice and peace. Being a Christian or Muslim today should mean simply learning to live according to the attitude of submission (islam). It should not mean necessarily becoming a member of an exclusive religious community.

If the generic concept called religion is indeed a modern invention, then by definition neither Jesus nor Muhammad could have been viewed as religious figures by their contemporaries. Where religion does not exist as a meaningful concept, religious-identity labels like Muslim, Christian, Jew are impossible to formulate. The obsession with religious identity today thus belies the vacuity of the very idea of religious identity. But then why *are* we so obsessed with empty religious-identity labels? Why do they persist? Because they stand as a largely failed attempt to allay the anxiety issuing from the demand to live from the perspective of a spiritually dead, superficial secular worldview. Nothing stands as a greater obstacle to the development of a deep and mature spirituality—and hence to the development of a responsible jihad—than the irresistible tide of secularism that has washed over the world in recent generations. Understanding the connection between secularism, religious identity, and spirituality will be a crucial part of any attempt to wage a responsible jihad.

THE QUEST FOR A MATURE SPIRITUALITY

I will begin by stating the obvious: Developing a mature spirituality can only occur in an environment where it is possible to believe that some sort of spiritual reality actually exists. The very word *spirituality* implies the ability to connect at a deep visceral level to a reality transcending the inanimate material world of atoms, molecules, and energy—the physical stuff of the universe. Unfortunately, the ability to make this type of deep spiritual connection is rapidly declining as a rising tide of secularism washes over the world, drowning the last vestiges of spiritual enchantment in the flood waters of scientific materialism. As I mentioned in an earlier chapter, the philosopher Charles Taylor, in his 800-page magnum opus *A Secular Age*, argues that the optional nature of belief in God, the gods, or any other type of spiritual reality is the defining feature of what we mean today by secularism. Five hundred years ago, Taylor says, an atheistic or purely materialist worldview would have been unthinkable for the vast majority of people. The existence of spiritual reality was as taken for granted as the daily rising and setting of the sun. Now, belief in God is just a choice one makes and is a difficult option to exercise for increasing numbers of people. In some ways, the secular worldview has now become the default option; the burden has shifted to the more spiritually minded to prove that belief in God or the gods is not irrational or antiscientific.

This turn toward scientific materialism is not difficult to see; the evidence is all around us. Consider, for example, how a common human experience that we have all likely had at one time or another is currently being reframed by the prophets of secularism. Taylor describes this experience with the words, "Somewhere, in some activity, or condition, lies a fullness, a richness; that is, in that place (activity or condition), life is fuller, richer, deeper, more worth-while, more admirable, more what it should be."[6] Taylor has in mind here the kind of experience where we seem to be lifted out of the plane of mundane, ordinary existence into a realm of timelessness and awe. Such an experience could result from things like seeing a beautiful sunset painted across the sky, hearing a musical performance that moves

6. Taylor, *Secular Age*, 5.

us to tears, or becoming so absorbed in an athletic activity that we lose all sense of time and place. I still remember the first time I encountered a bear in the wild (the summer of 1992 while hiking in Shenandoah National Park); I was transfixed and lost all sense of where I was or how much time had elapsed during this chance encounter. If such an experience occurs in a church, synagogue, mosque, or other sacred place, we might refer to it as a religious experience.

Though we have probably all had such memorable experiences, Taylor observes that our interpretation of these experiences has drastically changed. It used to be that a person coming to a place where "life is fuller, richer, deeper, more worthwhile, more admirable, more what it should be" might understand this experience as resulting from authentic connection to some unseen but nevertheless genuine spiritual reality. But today, the profound meaning of such an experience is more likely to be dismissed as the mere side effect of neural activity buzzing around in a material brain. In Taylor's words, "we have moved from a world in which the place of fullness was understood as unproblematically outside of or 'beyond' human life, to a conflicted age in which this construal is challenged by others who place it (in a wide range of different ways) 'within' human life."[7] While we continue to have experiences of fullness, their meaning has changed dramatically. If our experiences of fullness are nothing more than sensations created by particular patterns of brain activity, then it obviously no longer makes any sense to consider them as representing authentic connection to a spiritual reality transcending the world of ordinary matter. For Taylor, this move to interpret all experiences as arising from within the material structures of matter and energy is a chief characteristic of our secular age.

What has really occurred, I believe, is a fundamental crisis of confidence. We have lost confidence in our intuitive ability to discern aspects of reality through direct experience, instead placing all our confidence in empirical science as the only avenue to truth. In the secular world, only what can be empirically verified can be considered real. Since spiritual reality if it exists will by definition be immaterial, it can never be empirically verified and therefore bears no claim to being accepted as genuine. As a result, spirituality has for the most part been relegated to the category of superstition. Now, there is nothing wrong in principle with science; it can tell us profound truths about the nature of physical reality. For sure we cannot pillory the power of science (as some religious fundamentalists do) and

7. Ibid., 15.

then pull out our smartphones, iPads, computers, and all manner of technological wizardry brought to us by scientific investigation. The problem is not science itself but the tendency to elevate science to the vaunted position of truth's sole arbiter. Such an empiricist bias cannot be empirically verified! There is no laboratory experiment that could possibly verify the truth of the statement: all phenomena can be explained as resulting from natural laws acting on matter and energy. Such a statement is a philosophical proposition known as scientism; it is manifestly not science.

Be that as it may, neuroscience ignores this empiricist bias and continues apace trying to map the brain and reduce all feelings, emotions, and other subjective mental states to particular patterns of neural activity—activity that can then be quantified and displayed by an imaging device. Truth be told, the brain doctors have been quite successful at this, developing detailed maps of neural patterns that correlate well with a variety of particular subjective states. We can literally see a happy brain or a depressed brain. But the brain doctors have failed to ask the most fundamental question: how do the inanimate structures of the brain know to produce a mental state consistent with what is going on in a person's life? How does the brain (if it is merely made of atoms, molecules, and energy) know to produce a neural pattern consistent with the feeling of sadness when a boyfriend or girlfriend dumps us? It is not as if these neural patterns occur randomly. People generally don't experience happiness when a loved one dies, or sadness upon winning the lottery. The fact that researchers can produce particular mental states by artificially stimulating certain areas of the brain is not proof that these mental states are *caused* by the correlated patterns of neural activity. Correlation does not prove causation. We must rather answer the question, how are neural patterns consistent with the feelings and emotions appropriate to our life circumstances produced outside of the lab when the electrodes are disconnected and the imaging device is turned off?[8] I am not aware of a good empirically based answer to this question.

I realize this discussion may seem a bit abstract, so let me try to make it more concrete. Consider the following scenario: I am walking down the street feeling relaxed and happy after just having received a raise from my boss. Suddenly I am approached by a man who pulls a gun and demands my wallet. Immediately my sunny disposition transforms into a sense of dread and panic. But why? An imaging device might show a sudden switch

---

8. A critique of the excesses of brain science has recently been published: Satel and Lilienfeld, *Brainwashed*.

in the neural pattern in my brain from one consistent with happiness to one producing feelings of dread and panic, but this doesn't explain anything. We need to understand how the inanimate structures of matter and energy composing my brain are able to interpret the light rays emanating off the gunman and so to know that a neural pattern that produces feelings of dread and panic is more appropriate to my changed circumstances than one producing feelings of happiness. The visual stimulus of the man with the gun is really nothing more than an inanimate array of photons streaming through the lens of my eye and landing on my retina. The electrical stimulus produced then runs along my optic nerve to visual centers in my brain in order to produce a subjective image of the gunman. But how does an inanimate brain know that one type of visual stimulus *means* danger while another *means* peace? No one really knows how inanimate matter and energy achieve this trick, maybe because they don't. We must consider the possibility that an immaterial mind exists independent of the physical brain that acts as the interpretive agency overseeing the physiological activity of the brain. After all, we know that interpretation is an activity engaged in by minds, not matter. Rocks don't interpret; people do. So why shouldn't we consider that our minds exist somehow independent of our physical brains? If an immaterial mind does exist independent of the physical structures of the brain, then reality must be more than just physical stuff, and a way opens to reengage the possible existence of some form of spiritual reality. Unfortunately, few scientists are ready to accept this possibility even though they admittedly cannot provide an empirical explanation for how physical stuff generates our subjective mental experience.

This is sometimes known as the "hard problem" of science, and it continues to vex our greatest minds. One such mind belongs to David Barash, a highly influential evolutionary psychologist, who calls the problem of mind the hardest problem in science. According to Barash, "the hard problem of consciousness is so hard that I can't even imagine what kind of empirical findings would satisfactorily solve it. In fact, I don't even know what kind of discovery would get us to first base, not to mention a home run."[9] Interestingly, Barash's despair at solving the problem of mind and consciousness belies that fact that he seems to know the basic contours of such a solution already, for he describes himself as "an utter and absolute, dyed-in-the-wool, scientifically oriented, hard-headed, empirically insistent, atheistically committed materialist, altogether certain that matter and

9. Barash, "Hardest Problem in Science?"

energy rule the world, not mystical abracadabra."[10] Nevertheless, Barash writes, "I still can't get any purchase on this 'hard problem,' the very label being a notable understatement."[11] Perhaps this would lead Barash to adopt a position of epistemological humility, questioning whether his materialist bias is founded upon solid evidence. No such luck! He instead concludes, "I am convinced that . . . mind arises from nothing more nor less than the actions of the brain."[12] So much for humility! Barash is completely committed to a materialist solution that he admittedly has no empirical evidence for. This is a most brilliant display of philosophical scientism at work.

Barash's blindness to the possibility of transcendence would be humorous if it were not so tragic. He is simply acting on the scientistic (not scientific!) worldview that pervades the Western world (and due to globalization, increasingly the rest of the world). This worldview renders any sense of connection to a spiritual realm harder and harder to accept and leaves us in a disenchanted world of matter and energy. Such a world is permeated with the lost sense of meaningful life that flows from a superficial rather than authentic spirituality.

Nowhere does this scientistic tendency have a more tragic impact on life than in the perpetuation of the medical model of mental illness, to borrow a term from psychiatrist Elio Frattaroli. If the mind is simply a side effect of brain activity, then emotional disorders like anxiety and depression must have primarily physical causes and should therefore be treated like physical diseases. What happens when your body does not produce enough insulin, leaving you diabetic? You take insulin. Likewise, if your brain is not producing enough of the neurotransmitter serotonin, leaving you depressed, you take medication designed to boost the levels of serotonin in your brain to relieve the depression. Modern psychiatry has been transformed into a prescription-writing discipline, with few psychiatrists providing any kind of psychotherapy anymore. This is all fine as long as the medical model and its materialist assumptions are correct. But what if they're not?

A strong pushback against the medical model has been developing among psychiatrists and psychologists who recognize the dehumanization inherent in reducing people's deepest emotional and spiritual crises to the level of brain chemistry. Elio Frattaroli's *Healing the Soul in the Age of the*

10. Ibid.

11. Ibid.

12. Ibid.

Brain calls for a recovery of the old Freudian form of psychotherapy. Robert Whitaker's *Anatomy of an Epidemic: Magic Bullets, Psychiatric Drugs, and the Astonishing Rise of Mental Illness in America* wrestles with the striking paradox that rates of mental illness have skyrocketed in America since the beginning of the psychopharmacology revolution in the early 1980s. Once Prozac flooded the market, more people became depressed, not fewer! Whitaker provides a compelling argument that antidepressant medications may be doing more harm than good and should not be replacing nonmedical forms of mental-health intervention for many who live with depression. There appears to be no good scientific evidence that depressed people have lower levels of serotonin in their brains. This rather seems to be a tragic societal myth designed in part to fatten the coffers of the pharmaceutical industry at the expense of suffering people. As one more example, Gary Greenberg's *The Book of Woe: The DSM and the Unmaking of Psychiatry* documents the political and subjective nature of mental illness categories as they have been developed, revised, abandoned, expanded, recovered, only to be abandoned again in the various editions of the Diagnostic and Statistical Manual of Mental Disorders, the Bible of the psychiatric industry (and it is an industry!).

Despite all the fancy diagnostic gymnastics psychiatrists go through and the bevy of psychotropic medications at their disposal, there continues to be an epidemic of anxiety and depression in American society, with the astonishing number of thirty thousand to forty thousand suicides a year. This should not be accepted as normal but rather as the canary in the coal mine. Modern life is unhealthy both physically (as seen in epidemic levels of diabetes and heart disease) and mentally. Secularism has cut us off from deep spiritual roots and left us adrift in a sea of materialistic meaninglessness. It's no wonder we are all anxious and depressed. We may turn to our religious traditions to try and recover this lost sense of meaning, but religious people commit suicide at rates as high or higher than atheists, so religion does not appear to be the solution. This should come as no surprise. As long as we are caught up in our obsession with superficial religious-identity labels, we are bowing to the gods of secularism. Religious identity is the cousin of secularism. Religious communities today are likely full of functional atheists, people who make an intellectual confession of belief in God or the gods, but fail to really experience the reality of the spiritual at a deep visceral level. Secularism has hollowed out our religious traditions, leaving them impotent in the face of materialistic philosophy. To develop a mature spirituality, it is urgent that we transcend religious-identity labels and human-created dogmas.

While I have already argued that Jesus and Muhammad are good role models for doing this, we might also look to the work of the Swiss psychoanalyst Carl Jung for direction. Jung was absolutely convinced that the human psyche possessed a nearly infinite depth that connected in some mysterious way to the transcendent powers of the universe. He called this mysterious depth the Self and labeled our normal conscious understanding of ourselves the ego. The ego, for Jung, does not represent our true identity. The ego consists of a bevy of provisional identities acquired over the course of life as we interact with parents, siblings, and peers. These provisional identities may be functional or dysfunctional, depending on the nature of our relationships. If our parents abused us in some way, we will likely come to see ourselves as unlovable and deserving of abuse. If our parents constantly tell us we can never do wrong, on the other hand, we may develop an inflated sense of self-worth and become narcissistic brats. In neither case do these provisional identities represent who we truly are. They merely represent the sense we have developed of ourselves based on the environment in which we are raised, though we can be so unconscious of the provisional nature of these identities that we take them as real and behave accordingly. (This is why so many of us repeatedly engage in self-defeating behaviors.)

Eventually (often around middle age), Jung says, the Self demands expression and engineers a crisis in the form of an episode of anxiety or depression, or both—an episode that drives us to abandon our provisional identities and to connect to a deeper sense of self in order to survive the emotional crisis. Jung writes:

> I have frequently seen people become neurotic when they content themselves with inadequate or wrong answers to the questions of life. They seek position, marriage, reputation, outward success or money, and remain unhappy and neurotic even when they have attained what they are seeking. Such people are usually confined within too narrow a spiritual horizon. Their life has not sufficient content, sufficient meaning. If they are enabled to develop into more spacious personalities, the neurosis generally disappears.[13]

Jung suggests that the cure for anxiety and depression is not a prescription for antidepressants but a radical opening up of our sense of identity allowing us to connect deeply with the transcendence of the universe, provided we

13. Jung, *Memories, Dreams, Reflections*, 140.

can come to believe that such transcendence is real. This is no easy task. But to the extent that superficial religious-identity claims function as provisional identities in a secular world, Jung provides us with a compelling reason why transcending them is crucial for the development of a mature spirituality.

My own experience resonates strongly with this Jungian understanding of the nature of the psyche. I walked through the dark valley at midlife in the throes of a full-blown identity crisis that nearly crippled me with anxiety and depression, and it was only in discovering this Jungian paradigm that I was able to recover. Traditional religious formulations and medications were powerless to help. I needed to transcend my provisional identities—including my religious identity—and connect viscerally to the mysterious depths of my soul to discover my true identity. I wrote about this experience in *Radically Open: Transcending Religious Identity in an Age of Anxiety*. The point here is that I no longer consider myself a Christian even though I am still an active member of a Methodist church where I preach on occasion. I am a child of the universe who happens to find useful resources for my spiritual development within the so-called Christian tradition as well as in the Muslim tradition, the Buddhist tradition, and other traditions. Christianity is not an identity for me. I have transcended human-created institutional structures (even though I still participate in them) and derive my identity from something deeper. It is clear that Jesus and Muhammad had already accomplished this many centuries ago. This is the secret to developing the kind of mature spirituality without which there can be no responsible jihad. Are there contemporary models for this in Islam and Christianity? Indeed there are, and I would like to hold up the examples of Israr Ahmad and, once again, Walter Rauschenbusch.

Israr Ahmad

Though I never met him, I feel a sort of indirect personal connection to Israr Ahmad. Born in 1932 in India, Ahmad trained initially as a medical doctor before coming under the influence of Maulana Mawdudi, a well-known teacher of Islamic revivalism who had founded the Jama'at-i-Islami in 1941, a movement designed to spark a revival of Islam in South Asia and around the world. Ahmad joined the Jama'at movement in 1950 but left it in 1957 to begin his own work of reviving Islam. He eventually founded his own movement in 1975 under the name Tanzeem-e-Islami, and expanded this in 1993 with the creation of the Tanzeem-e-Islami in North America (or TINA). In 2003, Israr Ahmad passed leadership of TINA to Mustapha Elturk, and the organization's name was changed to the Islamic Organization of North America (IONA). As I mentioned previously, I have had the privilege to work closely with Ameer Mustapha and IONA, so I do feel as though I have an indirect connection to Israr Ahmad, who died in 2010. (Ameer Mustapha told me that they presented a copy of my earlier book *Was Jesus a Muslim?* to Dr. Ahmad before his death, and upon reading it, he wondered why I hadn't converted to Islam!)

What was Israr Ahmad's view of Islamic revivalism, and why did he leave Mawdudi's Jama'at movement? Ahmad believed that there were three obligations that Muslims owed God: personal submission, taking the message of Islam to others, and establishing Islam. He emphasized the comprehensive nature of Islam whereby Islam could not be understood simply as a religious movement of individual piety (personal submission); it had to entail the effort to bring all aspects of society (political, economic, social) in submission to God as well. Of course, transforming society in this way would require a jihad.

Now, by framing his work as the effort to create an Islamic revival, Israr Ahmad is admitting that this vision of Islam as a comprehensive system is not embodied in the world at present; it must be revived. According to Ahmad, the sad history of Islam in the modern period is its loss of any authentic, concrete embodiment in the world. He visualizes the three obligations to God as a three-storied building. The confession of faith—the Shahadah—is the foundation. The other pillars—prayer, *zakat*, fasting, pilgrimage—constitute the pillars that rest on the foundation of the Shahadah and in turn support the superstructure of the building—Islam— the comprehensive political, economic, and social system for all of life. But Ahmad laments the loss of this top floor, which has disappeared as Islam in the modern world has been reduced to nothing more than the pillars. He quips, "Let us not miss the obvious point that a structure having only pillars can at best be regarded as ruins of a bygone era."[14] With Islam no longer functioning as a comprehensive system for life, it has devolved to being nothing more than a religious identity. The comprehensive nature of Islam must be revived through jihad. But how exactly should one go about this?

Ahmad's interest in the revival of Islam explains his attraction to the Jama'at movement founded by Mawdudi, for Mawdudi too was motivated by the interest to revive Islam as a comprehensive system in the modern

14. Ahmad, *Obligations to God*, 30.

world. Initially, Mawdudi was committed to an Islamic revival based around the reeducation of Muslims who had forgotten what Islam really means and had been driven by the forces of secularism into an Islam-as-identity mindset. Ahmad comments, "Though there are now hundreds of millions of Muslims, in the word of the Prophet Muhammad (p.b.u.h.), they are like jetsam on the surface of the flood water having no value or substance. Our practice of Islam and fidelity and adherence to Qur'an has reached the state predicted by the Holy Prophet (p.b.u.h.) in the following Hadith: 'There will come a time when nothing will remain in Islam except its name.'"[15] Mawdudi and Ahmad both believed that reeducation of Muslims about the comprehensive nature of Islam was the foundation for any kind of revivalist movement. However, after the creation of the state of Pakistan in 1947, the Jama'at movement became politically active, trying to create an Islamic society in Pakistan directly through electoral politics. In the bargain, Ahmad claims, the Jama'at was "forced to compromise on principles and sometimes altogether sacrifice its pure Islamic ideals for political expediency."[16] Ahmad became convinced that the use of direct political power to transform society could not work if the people had not first been reeducated, so he left the Jama'at to focus on building the foundation for an authentic Islamic revival from the bottom up.

For Ahmad, the foundation for such a revival is faith (*iman*). But this faith is not merely intellectual assent to a set of doctrines; it is a deep inward connection to spiritual reality. Ahmad writes:

> The first step towards attaining this faith is to believe more firmly in some truths even though they are not observable or perceptible, and to hold the things heard by the heart to be more trustworthy than the things heard by the ear. Belief in the unseen is the first and foremost condition of *Iman* and this requires a radical change in the thought system and in the point of view of the believer.[17]

A true Islamic revival cannot be built on a foundation of functional atheism. One must reject the premise of secularism and be able to deeply engage the reality of a transcendent dimension to the cosmos. Without this authentic spiritual connection, Islam will devolve into a superficial religious-identity marker, leaving us with the silencing of the prophetic voice as we experience it today. Ahmad is adamant on this point: "Let it be clearly and distinctly

15. Ahmad, *Rise and Decline*, 15.

16. Ibid., 27.

17. Ahmad, *Islamic Renaissance*, 20.

understood that unless and until a major portion of the Muslim *Ummah* really undergoes this profound transformation in thought and belief, the vision and the fond hope of an Islamic renaissance can never be realized."[18]

Ahmad's vision of an Islamic revival contrasts sharply with much of what we witness in the world today, where jihad gets conflated with terrorism, and too many Muslims focus on political and legal methods of forcing Islamic dictates on a society of secularized people who lack the deep emotional connection to Allah described by Ahmad. Perhaps the contrast is most pronounced in the humility with which Ahmad approaches his work. He writes, "I will narrate my understanding of the duties of a Muslim. By so doing I do not rule out the possibility that my understanding is imperfect."[19] Imagine such an expression of humility coming from an apologist like Zakir Naik! Apologists are convinced they have all the answers and never admit to the possibility of ignorance. The ability to entertain doubt is an unmistakable sign of Ahmad's deep faith and authentic spiritual maturity. The dogmatism of religious fundamentalists is an admission of the superficiality of their faith. Deep faith is the only foundation on which a responsible jihad can be built, and Israr Ahmad is a shining example of what is possible.

He has certainly left his mark on his followers. I have been constantly impressed with the spiritual depth, humility, and outstanding hospitality displayed by all the members of IONA as I have come to know and work with them over the last several years. They truly embody the spirit of Israr Ahmad's teachings; I can personally attest that they are people of a deep and authentic faith. But such a faith is difficult to develop when we are surrounded by a sea of secularism that constantly disparages the notion of spiritual reality. Even someone like Israr Ahmad is not entirely immune to the effects of superficial religiosity, for even he can perpetuate the stereotype about an inherently violent Islam by pointing out how the followers of Muhammad "sallied forth like a flood from the Arabian peninsula with the Qur'an in one hand and a sword in the other";[20] he further describes how the Turkish armies, "after trampling all of eastern Europe under their feet, were knocking at the gates of Vienna."[21] Transcending our obsession with religious-identity labels that leads to violence is no minor achievement. It will require our full commitment.

18. Ibid., 21.

19. Ahmad, *Obligations to God*, 7.

20. Ahmad, *Rise and Decline*, 7.

21. Ibid., 5.

JESUS AND JIHAD

Walter Rauschenbusch

If any Christian in the modern era has been able to transcend Christianity as an identity label and fully engage its revolutionary political message it is Walter Rauschenbusch. As I briefly mentioned in an earlier chapter, Rauschenbusch, born in 1881, became a Baptist pastor serving a poor congregation in the Hell's Kitchen neighborhood of New York City during a turn-of-the-century America steeped in high levels of income inequality and economic injustice. Preaching the Christian gospel message of individual salvation failed to address the real needs of his congregation, given that his parishioners needed food to eat, clothes to wear, and access to health care. What good would it do them to know that their sins were forgiven if they were hungry, naked, and suffering? Rauschenbusch became convinced that a Jesus who had no relevance to the material needs of his parishioners had no relevance at all, and he began to preach a prophetic message critiquing the political and economic institutions responsible for the misery of his congregants.

Rauschenbusch, interestingly, recognized Jesus as a political figure engaged in a movement of resistance to the injustices authorized by the Roman Empire nearly a century before New Testament scholars made this discovery. As Rauschenbusch reread the Bible from the Old Testament prophets through the Gospels, he recognized that the biblical witness is not primarily about individual salvation but rather constitutes a powerful call for the creation of a divinely ordered world of social and economic justice. In 1907, he published the classic statement of his views in *Christianity and the Social Crisis*, a book that took the church by storm in the early decades of the twentieth century and continues to be as relevant today as it was the day it rolled off the presses.

One of Rauschenbusch's chief complaints about institutionalized Christianity is its transformation of the prophetic Jesus of the Gospels into a spiritualized figure presenting no threat to the powers of the status quo. In his inimitable style, Rauschenbusch writes:

> Imagine Jesus, with the dust of Galilee on his sandals, coming into the church of St. Sophia in Constantinople in the fifth century, listening to *dizzy* doctrinal definitions about the relation of the divine and human in his nature, watching the priests performing gorgeous acts of worship, reciting long and set prayers, and

offering his own mystical body as a renewed sacrifice to their God! Has anyone ever been misunderstood as Jesus has?[22]

Rauschenbusch keyed on the preeminence of the proclamation of the coming of the kingdom of God in Jesus's teaching, recognizing that as eternal life "came to the front in Christian hope, the kingdom of God receded to the background, and with it went much of the social potency of Christianity."[23] Rauschenbusch was acutely aware of the political nature of Jesus's proclamation of the kingdom and its relevance for modern constructions of Christian life. Christian identity is defined not by a longing for eternal salvation but by one's willingness to struggle for the realization of the kingdom on earth. Rauschenbusch, of course, does not use the word, but his understanding of the nature of Jesus's ministry is well captured by the term *jihad*.

Rauschenbusch worked tirelessly to call the church back to this jihadist mentality, a mentality it had lost through its obsession with formalistic ritual, theological speculation, and dogmatism. The church had lost its ability to think since

> dogmatism cooperated with ritualism, which likewise requires no intelligence in the worshiper, and which always acts as a narcotic on the intellect of people. But intellectual independence and determination are absolutely necessary if the moral forces are to make headway against deeply rooted wrongs."[24]

Rauschenbusch may not have won many friends by calling Christians stupid, but listening to the level of discussion that emanates from many Christian communities today suggests that Rauschenbusch was not too far off in his analysis! When Christians insist on a literal understanding of biblical creationism, deny the reality of global climate change, and ignore systemic economic injustice, Rauschenbusch's diagnosis appears prescient.

Of course, many churches would avow a concern for the poor and oppressed, a concern demonstrated by the considerable charity work that almost all churches engage in. Doesn't alleviating the suffering of the poor show a concern for economic injustice? In reply to this question I can only let Rauschenbusch speak for himself:

22. Rauschenbusch, *Christianity and the Social Crisis*, 82.
23. Ibid., 137.
24. Ibid., 149.

This is the stake of the churches in modern poverty. They are buried at times under a stream of human wreckage. They are turned aside constantly from their more spiritual functions to "serve tables." They have a right, therefore, to inquire who is unloading this burden of poverty and suffering upon them by underpaying, exhausting, and maiming the people. The Good Samaritan did not go after the robbers with a shotgun, but looked after the wounded and helpless man by the wayside. But if hundreds of Good Samaritans traveling the same road should find thousands of bruised men groaning to them, they would not be such very Good Samaritans if they did not organize a vigilance committee to stop the manufacturing of wounded men. If they did not, presumably the asses who had to lug the wounded to the tavern would have the wisdom to inquire into the causes of their extra work.[25]

It is not enough to provide assistance to the victims of an unjust economic system. One must inquire into why the system is set up in such a way as to create a class of poor people in the first place, and the system then needs to be transformed to eliminate poverty at its source. This will require a jihad.

There is no middle ground for Rauschenbusch. "The Church must either condemn the world and seek to change it, or tolerate the world and conform to it. In the latter case it surrenders its holiness and its mission. The other possibility has never been tried with full faith on a large scale."[26] Perhaps then it is time to try. If Walter Rauschenbusch, who as a pastor and a seminary professor was fully committed to the church, was nevertheless able to transcend the need to hold to a narrowly conceived Christian-identity label and fully engage the prophetic heart of Jesus, there is no reason why Christians today cannot do the same. And there is every reason to think that they must. There is too much at stake not to confront the pathology of Religious-Identity Obsession Syndrome. Christians need to finally throw superficial religious-identity labels aside and stand with Muslims and others in waging a responsible jihad against all the structures of oppression and exploitation that permeate the world.

In the final chapter, I will consider how waging a responsible jihad could help both Muslims and Christians reclaim their prophetic hearts and stand together in resistance to the economic, racial, gender, and environmental injustices that form an all too familiar part of life in the twenty-first century.

25. Ibid., 248.
26. Ibid., 274.

6

Reclaiming the Prophetic Heart of Christianity and Islam

*It is my conviction that if we are neutral in situations of injustice,
we have chosen the side of the oppressor.*

—Archbishop Desmond Tutu

It is incumbent upon every Christian and Muslim who does not wish to be neutral in situations of injustice to fully embrace jihad. To not do so is to forfeit a prophetic heart and become a tacit supporter of the unjust status quo. For as Archbishop Tutu's comment implies, there really is no neutral ground in situations of injustice. To not actively resist is to perpetuate. We must make a choice. Jesus clearly made that choice, for the evidence is clear that he was not a religious figure of individual piety in first-century Roman Palestine but a political figure of resistance to the injustices authorized by the Roman imperial system. In short, Jesus waged jihad. So, contrary to popular opinion, connecting Jesus with jihad is not heretical. Making this connection constitutes the recovery of the missing prophetic heart of the Christian tradition. Equating Jesus with jihad will only be controversial for those Christians so obsessed with superficial religious-identity labels that they have become deaf to the prophetic call for justice crying out from every corner of the contemporary world. This *is* an awful lot of Christians, to be sure. But for those able to see beyond the narrowness and superficiality of religious-identity labels and who can embrace an expanded vision of a world of justice and peace lived in authentic connection to a transcendent spiritual reality, jihad will be a crucial aspect of any attempt to reclaim the prophetic heart of not only Christianity but of Islam as well.

But why do we need to *reclaim* a prophetic heart? We normally need to reclaim only what has been taken from us, as when we reclaim stolen property. Has the prophetic heart of Christianity and Islam been stolen? By whom? The culprit is not any one person or group—no need to engage in a conspiracy theory here. The prophetic thief is simply the mutually reinforcing processes of secularization and religionization that are systematically running roughshod over any attempt to fully embrace the connection between the spiritual and the political.

Recall our earlier discussion of the work of Timothy Fitzgerald, who argues that the sacred/secular binary worldview so characteristic of the West authorizes the exploitative nature of global capitalism by creating an artificial distinction between facts and values. The economic system of the secular world is said to operate according to facts because values have been safely cordoned off in the religious realm where they become "objects of nostalgia" with no practical influence on the mundane affairs of life. The first order of business, then, for Muslims and Christians wanting to reclaim a prophetic heart from the thieves of secularism will be to wage a responsible jihad against the perpetuation of this artificial religious/secular dichotomy.

This will be no easy task, for the religious/secular dichotomy is so deeply entrenched within the modern Western worldview that to question it will seem outrageous to most. After all, we know that reality is dichotomized in this way, that there is a religious realm whose existence is real and clearly distinct from the secular realm of everyday life. We all know that politics is politics and religion is religion and that we cannot mix the two without risking the denigration of both. We all know that religion is the way people answer the deep and abiding questions of life: Who are we? What is the purpose of life? What is the nature of reality? We all know that our personal spirituality is unique to us, that it helps us make sense of the circumstances of our individual lives, and that we should never employ religious reasons to defend our views on public policy. We all know that economics is an empirical science whose practitioners simply describe human behavior in a morally neutral way. Of course we all know these things because global forces of injustice and exploitation have a vested interest in making sure that we know them. But these truths that we all know are not truths at all; they are propaganda, pure and simple.

The evidence for this, while almost universally overlooked, is actually quite overwhelming. Early Jews, Christians, and Muslims as we have seen lacked any notion of religion as a separate realm of existence clearly distinct from the secular affairs of the mundane world. No word for religion exists in the languages of the Bible or in Classical Arabic. A sacred/secular binary worldview simply made no sense to these ancient people. God in the Bible is a fully political and military figure, fighting Israel's enemies and making law and public policy for his chosen people. But where is the spiritual God of personal piety in the Bible? There is barely a trace. For Muslim scholar Fazlur Rahman, "There is no doubt that a central aim of the Qur'an is to establish a viable social order on earth that will be just and ethically based."[1] I agree, and this leaves the spiritual Allah of personal piety barely noticeable. The early sources of both Islam and Christianity know nothing of a religious/secular dichotomy. God is the sovereign power over all that exists. To attempt to place politics and economics beyond the reach of divine influence, as secularism seeks to do (and religion tacitly accedes to), makes an absolute mockery of Christian and Muslim professions of the omnipotence and sovereignty of God. Secularism is based on human claims to sovereignty, on the power and authority of humans to rule over and exploit one another and the entire earth. But these human claims to sovereignty stand squarely against the fundamental teachings of both Islam and Christianity.

Therefore, great courage will be required of Christians and Muslims who would dare to wage a responsible jihad. They will need to stand firmly against the deeply entrenched societal myth of the sacred/secular dichotomy and its American reflection, church/state separation. They will need to transcend their obsession with superficial piety and transcend their trivial and self-serving interest in personal salvation or eternal life to meet a God who calls them to communal concerns and social transformation. And they will need to respond to God's call for justice in ways that do not perpetuate further injustice. Now, the winners in the global capitalist economic system would naturally prefer that Christians and Muslims simply hold to their safe, depoliticized notions of personal spirituality, leaving political and economic concerns to the capitalist masters. But Muslims

---

1. Rahman, *Major Themes of the Qur'an*, 37.

and Christians must not remain on the sidelines and silent any longer. The stakes are too high. A responsible jihad must be waged and a prophetic voice must be reclaimed for the good of all the earth's inhabitants—human and more than human alike.[2] In what follows, I will sketch out a vision for a responsible jihad, specifically in reference to global economic injustice, gender and racial injustice, environmental injustice, and the search for a just peace. Three-and-a-half billion people have the power to change the world if they can only set their artificially imposed differences aside and mobilize in solidarity against injustice in all its varied and disturbing forms. It is time for a responsible jihad.

WAGING A JIHAD FOR ECONOMIC JUSTICE

Why is there so much economic injustice in the world? Why do more than two billion people subsist on less than a dollar a day while the citizens of wealthy nations consume resources at a rate that is quickly rendering the planet uninhabitable? Why do one in five American children live in poverty in the wealthiest nation on earth while as many as 45 million Americans experience chronic food insecurity? More important, why do Muslims and Christians stand meekly by, allowing this travesty of justice to go unchallenged as they attend to their religious beliefs and rituals? The answers to these questions are undoubtedly varied and complex, but the situation of economic injustice just might not be as complicated as it appears on the surface. Inequalities of wealth occur for the simple reason that large numbers of people embrace wealth accumulation as the principle goal of life, and they devise all kinds of ingenious technologies to funnel wealth to themselves at the expense of the middle class and the poor. Since wealth equals power, wealth accumulation is driven by nothing more than the unchecked human ego's desire for influence and authority (think the Koch brothers or Sheldon Adelson, for example).

These ingenious technologies of wealth accumulation and wealth concentration are beautifully analyzed by Nobel Prize winning economist Joseph Stiglitz in his book *The Price of Inequality: How Today's Divided Society Endangers Our Future*. Stiglitz begins by observing that there are two ways

---

2. I allude here to the phrase "more than human world," introduced by ecological philosopher David Abram, who prefers to highlight what is unique and special about the other organisms with which we share the planet, and so avoids the more common phrase "nonhuman world."

to become wealthy: create wealth (in which case, everyone wins) or take wealth away from others (in which case, some win; some lose). Inequality is rising in America for the primary reason that fewer and fewer people are invested in the process of trying to create wealth for all; they instead are engaged full time in the process of developing a myriad of schemes to redistribute wealth away from the poor and into the pockets of the rich. Stiglitz dubs this process of upward wealth redistribution "rent seeking." Most people think of rent as money paid to a landlord for the privilege of living on the landlord's property. The landlord does not receive the rent in exchange for anything he or she does to create wealth or grow the overall economy. That is, rent is not really earned. You don't actually *do* anything to get it. You just have to own something that someone else is willing to pay you to use.

According to Stiglitz, the idea of rent has now moved far beyond the traditional understanding of money owed to landlords with "rent seeking" becoming the favorite pastime of corporate CEOs, bankers, and Wall Street traders who invent all kinds of ingenious schemes designed to make money without returning anything of value to the overall economy. That is, they seek to generate income "not as a reward to creating wealth but by grabbing a larger share of the wealth that would otherwise have been produced without their efforts."[3] Rent seeking is, in short, a program of upward wealth redistribution and wealth concentration, making it the very engine of economic injustice. Rent-seeking behavior is deeply entrenched in both the American and the global economies. Consider some examples.

One need look no further than the financial crisis of 2008. Why did the world economy nearly collapse in that fateful year? Because for decades the financial sector of the American economy had been taking advantage of the poor and uninformed by loaning them money to buy houses they clearly could not afford. And why did these lenders make all these risky mortgage loans? First, they assumed—wrongly, as it turned out—that housing prices would keep increasing. But, second, they knew they could avoid risk by chopping up these mortgages, repackaging them as investment instruments, and then selling them to hungry investors in the form of mortgage-backed securities. As the global demand for securitized mortgages increased, investment banks did everything they could to meet the demand by luring anyone who would listen into borrowing money regardless of their ability to repay. The financial crisis of 2008 was driven by the

3. Stiglitz, *Price of Inequality*, 32.

desire of very smart (but not very wise) people to make money without earning it. It was driven by rent seeking. Stiglitz considers these predatory lending practices along with abusive credit-card interest rates to constitute the most egregious forms of rent seeking in our society.[4] Notice how the rent seekers, because they play such an enormous role in the stability of the overall economy, got themselves bailed out only to return to their devious rent-seeking practices after the dust had settled. The middle class and poor paid and continue to pay the price in the form of stagnant wages, high unemployment and underemployment, and deterioration of the social safety net. This is the very definition of economic injustice.

Examples of rent-seeking behavior abound. The reason the proverbial top 1 percent of income earners has garnered almost all the increase in income over the last thirty years is that corporate CEO salaries have become staggeringly large due to rent seeking. The CEO of United Health Group received $102 million in 2010 while the CEO of Qwest Communications earned $65.8 million. Stiglitz makes clear that "it is not a sudden increase in their productivity that allowed these CEOs to amass such riches . . . but rather an enhanced ability to take more from the corporations that they are supposed to be serving."[5] The 2003 Medicare drug benefit passed by President Bush became a fifty-billion-dollar-per-year giveaway to an already wealthy pharmaceutical industry by virtue of the provision barring the federal government from bargaining for drug prices. The drug companies garner enormous profits without earning it; the rest of us pay the bill through our Medicare taxes. Wealth is systematically redistributed from middle-class and poor Americans upward to large corporations and their top executives.

The growth of rent-seeking behavior parallels, not surprisingly, the growth of the financial sector as a share of the total U.S. economy. Research shows that as the financial sector of an economy grows, wealth inequality grows with it.[6] This link is no accident. Government deregulation of the financial industry and government subsidies distort the economy, "not only leading to a larger financial sector but also enhancing its ability to move money from the bottom to the top."[7] Stiglitz concludes that much of the inequality in the U.S. economy results from rent-seeking behavior. "In their

4. Ibid., 37.
5. Ibid., 42.
6. Ibid., 81; Galbraith, *Inequality and Instability*.
7. Stiglitz, *Price of Inequality*, 81.

simplest form, rents are just redistributions from the rest of us to the rent seekers."[8]

It is fair to say that those Stiglitz dubs rent seekers would blanch at the ethically dubious manner in which he portrays their behavior. Is there another side to this story? Can rent-seeking behavior be justified? One popular form of justification involves reframing rents as incentives. People are motivated by money, and important people like corporate CEOs and bankers need large incentives to provide quality service. We heard this justification in the aftermath of the 2008 financial collapse when it was revealed that Wall Street firms were paying huge bonuses to their top level executives even though those executives had helped to nearly wreck the world economy. The firms had to pay these bonuses, we were told, in order to attract and hold onto top talent. Really? The architects of economic disaster are considered the best and brightest? So much for the attempt to justify rent seeking! But the very fact that this kind of outrageous argument is seriously made just shows how completely devoid of spiritual connection these barons of secularism have become. Ethical values have become so divorced from economic reality (as Fitzgerald predicts) that for the rent seekers, money is all that motivates them. How sad. As the saying goes, "Some people are so poor that all they have is money!"

I do not exaggerate here. In a 2013 interview in the *Wall Street Journal*, the CEO of AIG, the huge insurance conglomerate that was bailed out by taxpayers in 2008 to the staggering tune of $182 billion, compared the uproar over executive bonuses to pre–civil rights lynchings in the Deep South! Earlier, the CEO of Blackstone Group, a large international private-equity firm, compared proposals to close the carried-interest tax loophole to Hitler's invasion of Poland![9] What an outrageous insult to African Americans who felt the wrath of real lynch mobs and the people of Eastern Europe who directly experienced the terrors of Hitler. These corporate elitists have no shame and have lost all sense of perspective about what really matters in life. How does one even begin to respond to such outrageous nonsense. Words fail me!

For his part, Stiglitz reminds us just how ludicrous this is:

> The absurdity of incentive pay in some contexts is made clear by thinking of how it might apply to medical doctors. Is it conceivable that a doctor performing heart surgery would exert more care

8. Ibid., 95.

9. See Krugman, "Plutocrats Feeling Persecuted."

or effort if his pay depended on whether the patient survived the surgery or if the heart valve surgery lasts for more than five years? Doctors work to make sure each surgery is their absolute best, for reasons that have little to do with money.[10]

Do teachers teach for love of money? Do lawyers do pro bono work to get rich? Do airline pilots intentionally crash planes after their union loses a contract negotiation and their salaries are cut? Of course not. People, thankfully, are motivated by all sorts of incentives besides money. Just think of all those low-paid daycare workers out there (like my wife) who provide professional child care simply because of their love of children. It is the rent seekers who have lost all connection to authentic life. I could almost feel sorry for them if it wasn't for how their behavior brings so much misery to others. If rent seeking is a primary cause of economic injustice, how in the world can Christians and Muslims remain silent, unwilling to exercise a prophetic voice in the face of such unwarranted exploitation? How would Jesus act? What would Muhammad do?

Jesus and the Imperial Economy

There is clear evidence that Jesus resisted the exploitative actions of the Roman imperial economy. Rent seeking is not just a modern phenomenon; Roman imperial officials were rent seekers too. In fact, the whole point of an imperial economic system is to funnel resources and wealth from the edges of the empire into the imperial center for the benefit of the imperial elite, who accumulate vast riches without earning them (the definition of rent seeking). The Roman elite did not develop an economic system designed to provide for the material needs of all the inhabitants of their empire. They developed an economic system designed to benefit themselves at the expense of the subject peoples of the empire, of which Jesus was a part. And Jesus did not stand idly by in acceptance of this system while he preached a spiritual message of personal salvation. No! He led a movement of resistance against it.

As we saw earlier, the Jewish temple was the premier institution of Roman economic exploitation. The temple functioned as a Roman bank, siphoning off the wealth that collected there through an elaborate system of "religious" ritual obligations in order to pay for the expansion of the

10. Stiglitz, *Price of Inequality*, 109.

exploitative imperial apparatus. Jesus's crucifixion at the hands of Roman imperial officials seems to have occurred just days after he disturbed the efficient operation of this system by overturning the tables of the moneychangers and driving out those who bought and sold in the imperial economy. Jesus's rejection of and resistance to an unjust economic system was radically prophetic. So how can a contemporary Christian's resistance to the unjust rent-seeking behavior of the global capitalist elite be any less radical? To not resist is to perpetuate. Do Christians really want to be the supporters of injustice?

The Christian prophetic voice received a welcome boost in the fall of 2013 with the appearance of Pope Francis's apostolic exhortation *Evangelii Gaudium* (*The Joy of the Gospel*). Francis warned us of "the dictatorship of an impersonal economy lacking a truly human purpose." He explained that wealth inequality results from ideologies "which defend the absolute autonomy of the marketplace and financial speculation." He further warned that "the thirst for power and possessions knows no limits," while explaining that ethics are often seen as counterproductive because they render money and power relative. Finally, in order to allay fears that he is entirely antibusiness Pope Francis offers this sage advice:

> Business is a vocation, and a noble vocation, provided that those engaged in it see themselves challenged by a greater meaning in life; this will enable them truly to serve the common good by striving to increase goods of this world and to make them more accessible to all.[11]

Is Pope Francis a student of Joseph Stiglitz? For Pope Francis, the growing of wealth is acceptable as long as we grow it for everyone. But rent-seeking behavior that simply redistributes wealth upward must be vehemently resisted. All Christians—Catholic or otherwise—should embrace the prophetic spirit of the pope. Some Protestants will balk at any suggestion that a pope speaks the truth, but this is nothing more than Religious-Identity Obsession Syndrome at work. Truth is truth, no matter who speaks it, and Pope Francis, at least on the issue of economic injustice, has set the agenda for all Christians to follow who wish to reclaim a prophetic heart.

---

11. See especially paragraphs 56, 57, and 203 for Pope Francis's views on economics.

Muhammad and the Pagan Economy

Like Jesus, Muhammad also lived in a time marked by high levels of economic injustice. In the fractured tribal society of pre-Islamic Arabia, might made right, and wealth accumulated in the hands of the strong at the expense of the weak. Recall how Ja'far indicated to the king of Abyssinia that before the advent of Islam the strong devoured the weak. Clearly, one of the primary reasons warring tribes attacked each other was to exact tribute in order to enrich the winners. Not much sense in defeating an enemy if you don't siphon off all his wealth for yourself! Remember too that Muhammad's chief opposition, the Umayyads, had a direct economic interest in the polytheistic system of idol worship since they oversaw the pilgrimages to the Ka'ba and manufactured and sold the idols used for worship during these pilgrimages. How did Muhammad respond to this economic system and the injustices it authorized? Did he leave it intact and simply tell his followers to go observe the Five Pillars? Not exactly.

Muhammad instead declared submission to one God and actively stamped out the polytheistic idolatry of his people. This directly countered the tribal economic system, a system entirely incompatible with the idea of a unified humanity living in submission to one God. The drive of the human ego for power and wealth had now to be subordinated to the will of a deity who demanded justice, not exploitation; peace, not conflict. Muhammad's preaching was radically prophetic, not only in the way that Muslims usually interpret the term *prophetic* (coming directly from God), but also in the more general meaning of the word—challenging and disturbing the status quo. How can contemporary Muslims, then, not raise their voices in a unified chorus of protest against the global capitalist war on the poor? Jihad is incumbent upon every Muslim without exception.

In summary, we saw earlier that prophetic voices of economic critique do exist in both Christianity and Islam, but those voices are more the exception than the rule. They need to become the rule. How might this happen? It will not be enough to simply critique the current system. An entirely new system based on an alternative set of principles must be envisioned. I can think of no better example of fresh economic thinking than what is today called Islamic Economics. Under the banner of Islamic Economics, contemporary Muslim thinkers have been at work articulating a vision of an economic system that grows organically out of Islamic principles and that represents a system fundamentally different from both capitalism and socialism. Let's consider a few of the principles of Islamic economic thinking.

Islamic Economics

The spirit of Islamic Economics is best summed up in this extraordinary statement by Mustafa Mahmud:

> Wealth is not sought for itself in Islam but is sought as a means to piety and a way to upright, merciful, and loving action. This marks it as different from the meaning of wealth in materialist capitalist economy and materialist socialist economy. These latter look at wealth as economic power and as a means for domination and conquest. Activity without a spiritual sense is dry and lifeless.[12]

How different this principle is from the rent-seeking behavior of the capitalist elite! Wealth in Islam is not an end in itself, and therefore wealth accumulation cannot become the be all and end all of life. Wealth is merely a trust from God, a resource to be used for the creation of a just, merciful, and loving society that cares for all its people. So much for the theory of the capitalist masters that money is the only incentive to work!

Of course, an economic vision like Mahmud's would be highly ridiculed in a standard economics classroom. The very idea that wealth can function as a means to piety sounds utterly absurd to someone thoroughly invested in the religion/secular dichotomy. For them, *religion* is the sole means to piety; wealth is either an end in itself or a means to power but certainly not a means to piety. Since religion and economics address fundamentally different realms of life, they should never be confused or intermixed. This is the prevailing attitude anyway. But if we can recognize the artificiality of the religion/secular divide and its imbrication in the maintenance of unjust economic systems while firmly confessing the full sovereignty of God, it is only natural to recognize that an authentic economic system must be built on an ethic of mutual caring, not competitive greed, and that participating in the economic activity of such a system could assist in the development of religious piety. That is, living in such a system would socialize us into an ethic of cooperation and caring—characteristics we associate with piety—just as living in the capitalist system socializes us into an ethic of competition and greed. This is why Sayyid Qutb's view of jihad as a movement to transform institutions is so important. So much of how we view the world is influenced by the institutional structures in which we live. For people to change, institutions must change as well.

12. Mahmud, "Islam vs. Marxism and Capitalism," 131.

Another important Islamic economic thinker, M. Umar Chapra, has written, "It is the duty of the Islamic state to ensure a respectable standard of living for every individual who is unable to take care of his own needs and hence requires assistance."[13] This "respectable standard of living" is provided for by the third pillar of Islam—*zakat*. Recall that *zakat* entails the levying of an annual tax on accumulated wealth to be redistributed to the needy until they can be restored to productive life and become *zakat* payers rather than recipients. A *zakat* system would have the effect of smoothing out large disparities of wealth in the society while ensuring a life of basic dignity for all people. But the very notion of wealth redistribution from rich to poor is anathema to the capitalist elite, who spend their days devising all kinds of clever schemes to redistribute wealth from the poor to the rich. It is not wealth redistribution in principle that they are against; it is only the direction of redistribution that concerns them! For the capitalist elite, the state's overarching concern is not the ensuring of a respectable standard of living for every individual. The state functions to simply maintain the rigged economic playing field that serves the interest of unfettered capitalist wealth accumulation with a rapidly expanding underclass simply taken as the price of doing business.

Should we meekly accept this reality? Not if we listen to Tariq Ramadan:

> Islam does not conceive of poverty as a normal feature of the social arena and does not envisage that the remedy for this distortion should be the free generosity of some toward others in the hope that the wealth of the rich and the destitution of the poor may somehow miraculously find a point of balance. The obligation of *zakat* puts this question into the realm of law and morality and cannot be left to anyone's discretion. Social solidarity is part of the faith and is its most concrete testimony: to be with God is to be with people; this is the essence of the teaching of the third pillar of Islam.[14]

Accepting an economic system that creates poverty while depending on voluntary charity to alleviate the suffering of the victims is not an Islamic value, and it should not be understood as a Christian one either. Farid Esack agrees:

---

13. Chapra, "Islamic Welfare State," 242.
14. Ramadan, *Western Muslims and the Future of Islam*, 178.

> I would suggest that any religiosity which fails to see the connections between poverty and the socio-political structures which breed and sustain poverty and injustice but then hastens to serve the victims is little more than an extension of those structures, and therefore complicit in the original crime.[15]

To be Muslim is to resist economic injustice. But resisting economic injustice will require that we struggle against the powers of the unjust status quo. So to be Muslim by definition means to wage a jihad for economic justice. If Jesus was engaged in jihad, then the struggle for economic justice becomes incumbent upon Christians too.

How should Christians and Muslims go about this? Transforming a deeply entrenched global economic system will not be easy and may well be impossible. But its near impossibility is no excuse for meek acquiescence. Tariq Ramadan exhorts his fellow Muslims to develop alternative commercial structures and management systems "that will make it possible for them, in time, to extricate themselves from the logic with which the system and its dominating power force them for a while to comply."[16] For Ramadan, "our rejection of the dominant economic system is radical *by nature*. The reality that may force us to interact does not in any way force us to give up."[17]

Christians and Muslim have little choice but to live in and interact with the global capitalist system. But they can still question its ethics at every turn and refuse to shape their lives around its materialistic philosophy of consumption and greed. They can vote for and empower leaders who fight for economic justice (like Senators Elizabeth Warren and Bernie Sanders) and boycott corporations who engage in the worst abuses. There are many forms of nonviolent resistance and acts of civil disobedience that a jihad for economic justice can take. But their effectiveness will be directly proportional to the number of people involved. An effective jihad will require that Christians and Muslims stand together rather than in opposition to each other. Sadly, the current antipathy that divides so many Christians and Muslims only serves to reinforce the unjust status quo—all the more reason for the powers of the status quo to fan the flames of interreligious discord and Islamophobia—divide and conquer! It is time for Muslims and Christians to stand as one in demanding an economic system based

15. Esack, *On Being a Muslim*, 92.

16. Ramadan, *Western Muslims and the Future of Islam*, 198.

17. Ibid., 199.

on fairness and equality, not rent seeking and exploitation. Jihad is not a dirty word. It is the only appropriate response to the mournful cry of the economically oppressed.

WAGING A JIHAD
FOR GENDER AND RACIAL JUSTICE

Christians often like to emphasize the (in their view) miserable condition of women in the Muslim world in order to portray Islam as primitive and backwards. Since Christianity is a highly evolved religion, evangelizing primitive Muslims will help to free Muslim women from their oppression, the argument goes. The stereotype of the oppressed Muslim woman is, of course, problematic as there are many well-educated successful women in Muslim countries and quite a few oppressed ones in the West. Yet there certainly are places in the Muslim world where women do not enjoy the rights seemingly accorded them by Islamic sources. At the same time, one political party in "enlightened" America is systematically trying to roll back decades of progress in equal rights for women. Civil rights are under attack as well (especially the right to vote), so there are ample reasons for Christians and Muslims to wage a jihad for gender and racial justice.

In talking about gender and race we are back to talking about identity once again. Just as many are under the influence of Religious-Identity Obsession Syndrome, many people today are caught up in obsessive adherence to gender and racial norms that lead to the kinds of patriarchal and racist ideologies that cause so much strife and suffering in the world. Just as Christians and Muslims must learn to transcend their obsession with religious-identity labels, so they must also learn to embrace a common humanity that transcends obsessive concern with gender and racial identities. This does not mean that we cannot honor the evident differences between men and women, or that we seek to become color-blind. (Why would we even want to be color-blind? How boring!) But it does mean gender and racial differences must not be raised to the level of absolute identity, as if a woman's gender is so absolutized that it erases any trace of the particular talents, abilities, and intelligences that make her as much a unique human being as any man; or as if a person's race is allowed to efface the qualities that render a person a unique individual. The uniqueness of every woman in the world is more important than the fact of her membership in a group. Likewise for people who are black, Hispanic, Semitic, or of any other racial or ethnic identity. Fortunately, Islamic and Christian sources are full of exhortations to transcend a fixation on gender and race. We need to reengage these voices.

Muhammad and Jesus certainly provide good examples. Muhammad married a wealthy and powerful woman fifteen years his senior who had proposed marriage to him—hardly a patriarchal move. And evidence exists that a woman may have helped compile and edit the Qur'an.[18] Women played an important role in the movement spawned by Jesus and the Apostle Paul too (Paul even recognizes a woman by the title of Apostle in Romans 16!). The first person chosen to give the call to prayer by Muhammad was Bilal, an African (not an Arab). Jesus counsels acceptance of other racial and ethnic groups by telling the parable of the Good Samaritan. The struggle against patriarchal, xenophobic, and racist norms was a major part of the early Christian and Islamic movements. Therefore, the patriarchal and racist interpretations of both that dominate in the world today represent a tragic reversal of these progressive transformations.

When it comes to the struggle against racism Muslims have a particularly good record. The Islamic concept of *tawhid* (unity) which includes within its scope the unity of all humanity living in submission to one God has had the fortunate effect of raising one's identity as a Muslim to a level of greater importance than one's racial, ethnic, or national identity. The annual hajj pilgrimage to Mecca demonstrates this unity with millions of Muslims from every conceivable racial and ethnic background joining together in this great display of Muslim unity. It is well known that Malcolm X's transformation from a militant black nationalist to orthodox Muslim was in part inspired by his own hajj experience. During his pilgrimage to Mecca he failed to experience the kind of racism in this racially diverse group of Muslims that he experienced in America and reasoned that Islam might contain effective resources for combating racial injustice. Many of the mosques I have visited in America have been models of racial and ethnic diversity; much more so than American churches, which remain highly segregated. Yet despite this positive history, when it comes to race relations, it is indeed unfortunate to find a virulent strain of anti-Semitism still lurking in the hearts of far too many Muslims today. In a world where the infamous Ayatollah Khomeini, architect of the Iranian Revolution, could write the following, "From the very beginning, the historical movement of Islam has had to contend with the Jews, for it was they who first established

18. For more on this fascinating idea, see Khan, "Did a Woman Edit the Qur'an?"

anti-Islamic propaganda and engaged in various stratagems, and as you can see, this activity continues down to the present. Later they were joined by other groups, who were in certain respects more satanic than they," the struggle against particular forms of bias, prejudice, and intolerance is far from over in Islam.[19] Khomeini's is only a single voice, to be sure, but I fear such anti-Semitic sentiments are shared more commonly than we know, given the history of Israeli occupation of Palestinian lands. But speaking against Israeli political, social, and military policy does not require one to be anti-Semitic or anti-Jewish. Muslims must learn not to confuse espousing anti-Israeli policies and expressing anti-Semitism or anti-Judaism.

While the struggle for racial and ethnic justice is not over in Islam, in some ways it is just beginning in Christianity. Martin Luther King Jr. called eleven o'clock on Sunday morning the most segregated hour in America, and little has changed since the 1960s. The white church experience remains largely independent from the black church experience, and racial animus in American society is too often associated with self-identified Christian movements. For example, the Ku Klux Klan still marches, and the Internet is a veritable dung heap of white supremacist websites claiming Christian identity. But the problem is not just with these fringe groups. A much larger stream of racist attitude was unleashed in 2008 with the election of the country's first African American president. (The Southern Poverty Law Center reports a surge in the number of white-supremacist hate groups during the Obama presidency.[20]) The thinly veiled xenophobia of the Republican Party, which appears on the surface in the form of grotesquely distorted caricatures of the president's policy initiatives ("death panels," "anticonstitutional lawlessness") unfortunately enjoys many mainstream Christian supporters. (In many ways the Republican Party and evangelical Christianity are one and the same.) Many of these same Christian politicians resist a path to citizenship for undocumented workers, another obvious attempt to resist the well-documented "browning" of America. Christians, unfortunately, have a long way to go to meet the standard set by Jesus for transcending racial, ethnic, and national identities—a long way to go to recognize the full humanity of all people everywhere.

In some ways the situation may be getting worse with the development of Islamophobia over the last twenty years and especially since 9/11. High-profile Christians are some of the biggest perpetrators of anti-Muslim

19. Algar, *Islam and Revolution*, 27.
20. Southern Poverty Law Center, "Hate Group Numbers Up by 54% since 2000."

bigotry. Christian politicians (including President Obama; yes, he is a Christian, not a Muslim) support government programs that profile Muslim Americans (like Tareq Mehanna), subjecting them to preemptive prosecution and imprisonment even before they have committed any crime. Christians have been vocal opponents of mosque-building projects in various parts of the country. Islamophobia is just the latest strain of racism to infect a Christian church, which continues to deal with anti-Semitism and anti-black racism. Those Christians who do affirm the full dignity and humanity of all people everywhere (and there are a lot of them) need to stand in solidarity with Muslims on this issue. Large numbers of Christians and Muslims refusing to participate in racist structures and openly speaking out against them would be a powerful witness that the jihad for racial justice was underway.

There are signs of hope for Christians in this regard. Recently, an African American congregation affiliated with the United Church of Christ (UCC) began worshiping together with a predominantly white UCC congregation in Saint Paul, Minnesota. What drew them together? The pastor of the African American church, Rev. Oliver White, took a prophetic stand several years ago in his thriving black church in support of gay marriage. This unpopular position caused his church to dwindle from over three hundred members to nearly one hundred. Unable to financially support their community any longer, Rev. White's shrinking congregation sold their church building and sought another place of worship. A white congregation, under the leadership of Rev. Lisa Bodenheim (a congregation also supportive of gay marriage) offered the use of their building to Rev. White's congregation. But rather than worshiping at different times, the two congregations decided to worship together. Rev. White admits to a sense of wonder about how this arrangement came about, but on second thought says, "I [came] to realize, we're all people and if I can be an advocate for the LGBT community, then why can't I be an advocate for bringing people together in one accord, which is what I'm trying to do."[21] Rev. White is a shining example of a pastor not afflicted with Religious-Identity Obsession Syndrome (same for Rev. Bodenheim). A shared prophetic vision has overridden a common racial divide. We can only hope to see more of this.

When it comes to the issue of gender, one could argue that it is Christians who are ahead of Muslims. The movement toward equal rights for women has produced tangible progress both within Western society and

21. Quoted in French, "Grace Church Pastor."

within the church. Women are doctors, lawyers, corporate CEOs, and powerful politicians (though at the time of writing, not president), and they participate as ordained ministers in many (but not all) Protestant denominations. Of course, Muslim women serve as doctors, lawyers, university professors, and powerful politicians (even as prime ministers) too. Yet the truly egregious types of patriarchal behavior—honor killing, stoning, and female genital mutilation—that occur in some parts of the Muslim world would be unthinkable in the West. Despite the status accorded women in Islamic teachings (as the stabilizing forces in the household, and therefore in the society at large), women do appear to hold a secondary status in the worship life of Muslim communities—banned as they are from leading the prayers, and required as they are to remain hidden behind a screen or in a balcony. Particularly this separation of women from men in worship motivated the African American Muslim convert Amina Wadud to openly declare a "gender jihad."

Wadud has caused a stir by at least twice (once in South Africa and once in New York City) taking it upon herself to lead Friday prayers in a mosque. While many Muslims, both men and women, find Wadud's gender activism objectionable, the theoretical basis of her actions deserves consideration. Wadud defends her activism on the basis of what she calls the "*tawhidic* paradigm." Trading on the Islamic affirmation of the utter unity of God, Wadud argues that *tawhid* renders impossible any kind of hierarchical relationship that prioritizes men over women (or that would prioritize women over men, for that matter). In her view, *tawhid* allows for the existence of only a single hierarchical structure—that of God over everything else, because "the highest moral point is always occupied metaphysically by Allah."[22] The patriarchal interpretive practices that through the centuries have relegated women to secondary status violate this "*tawhidic* paradigm" by creating a secondary gender hierarchy under the divine/human hierarchy. Wadud thus concludes, "The overarching concept *tawhid*, or the unicity of Allah, forms a trajectory organizing Islamic social, economic, moral, spiritual, and political systems. All are under a single divine reality."[23]

Interestingly, Wadud's "*tawhidic* paradigm" accords very well with the work of Christian feminist biblical scholar Elisabeth Schüssler Fiorenza. Schüssler Fiorenza has coined the term *kyriarchy* to name the problem more familiarly known as patriarchy. From the Greek words for "lord"

22. Wadud, *Inside the Gender Jihad*, 30.
23. Ibid., 29.

(*kyrios*) and rulership (*arche*), *kyriarchy* names the human penchant for creating hierarchies of all kinds: man over woman, white over black, humans over nature. For Schüssler Fiorenza, the oppression of women does not stem primarily from a man-over-woman hierarchy (patriarchy) but from this deeper human desire for lordship (*kyriarchy*) more generally, and so feminist resistance must take on all hierarchical relationships in order to restore a world where all forms of life are understood as equal before God. Schüssler Fiorenza's critique of *kyriarchy* is strikingly reminiscent of Wadud's *tawhidic* paradigm, a point that should have the power to pull Muslims and Christians together in waging a gender jihad.

Wadud is not alone in her feminist activism even if she has been bolder in her actions. Many Muslim women around the world are engaged in the struggle against patriarchal interpretations of Islamic sources and the oppressive practices these interpretations authorize, and a specifically Islamic feminist movement has (or a variety of movements have) developed. One such feminist activist, Saʿdiyya Shaikh, exposes the hypocrisy whereby Muslim leaders "hold forth endlessly about the fact that Islam accords women high status and liberation while simultaneously promoting hierarchical and discriminatory power relationships between men and women."[24] The solution for the problem of hierarchical and discriminatory power relationships is not, however, the secularization of society as is the case for many Western secular feminists, but rather the recovery of an egalitarian form of Islam that can shape political, social, and economic structures in a just and equitable way. That is, Islamic feminists are Islamists. They reject the religious/secular dichotomy and argue that women's rights can only be secured within the bounds of divine reference. Reflecting on the flowering of Islamic feminist activism around the world, Shaikh concludes, "In the last analysis, Islamic feminism is, in my view, one of the most engaged contemporary responses to the core qur'anic injunction for social justice of our time."[25] Muslim women are exercising a prophetic voice. Are Muslim men listening?

Whether it be in the struggle for economic justice or the struggle for gender and racial justice, a responsible jihad must entail the large-scale rejection of the religious/secular dichotomy that secularizes the world and marginalizes divine reference in the most important spheres of life: the political, the economic, and the social. Secularism creates a world safe for

24. Shaikh, "Transforming Feminisms," 148.
25. Ibid., 159.

the ravenous desires of the human ego for material fulfillment, leading to rent seeking and exploitation. Secularism also cuts us off from authentic connection to spiritual reality, leaving us more vulnerable to the kinds of identity obsessions that lead to racism, xenophobia, and patriarchy. Enacting the *tawhidic* paradigm and its rejection of *kyriarchy* will go a long way toward taming the human ego and its drive for material accumulation and the hierarchical ordering of society. Perhaps the most visible and powerful form of jihad would be for Christians and Muslims to simply set an example for the world of what a deeply grounded authentic spirituality looks like. The incessant drive for wealth accumulation makes no one happy, and those disenchanted with life in our secular age would be drawn to authentic displays of mature spirituality. What a gift Christians and Muslims could bestow on a confused and hurting world if they could just reject all obsession with religious-identity labels and simply live lives of spiritual connection that transcend their differences and affirm the full human dignity of all people everywhere. This may be a grand utopian vision, I admit. But to consider its fulfillment impossible is to consign ourselves to a continuation of our current miseries and to an unsustainable future for all life on the planet. Is this a cost worth paying just to maintain our fixation on superficial piety? It is a devil's bargain. I recall someone named Jesus saying something about gaining the world but losing our souls! The stakes are so high that even our survival as a species might be threatened.

WAGING A JIHAD FOR ENVIRONMENTAL JUSTICE

Perhaps the most important of all global issues today is the permanent altering of the physical environment of the planet such that the continuation of life in all its forms is threatened. While many people are aware of issues like global climate change, loss of biodiversity, and pollution of the biosphere, few tend to think of these problems as issues of justice. This is unfortunate since basic issues of justice stand at the very heart of the human destruction of a livable environment. Let's make this explicit.

The reality of global climate change caused by human activity is about as solid a scientific consensus as there is, the naysayers notwithstanding. The production of greenhouse gasses from human energy consumption is raising the average temperature of the planet, melting glaciers and polar ice caps, and altering long-stable weather patterns, causing floods and droughts. But all humans across the planet are not equally responsible for the creation of this problem. Nor are all people equally affected by the consequences. People living in highly industrialized areas, including the United States, Europe, China, India, and Brazil, contribute substantially more to the warming of the atmosphere than do those who live in less developed parts of South America, Africa, and Asia. Yet the less developed nations have access to far fewer resources to combat the effects of climate change on their populations. Despite the hardships of the Dust Bowl days in America, there was still enough of a functional safety net in place to prevent the mass starvation of Americans. But prolonged droughts in East Africa in recent decades have killed hundreds of thousands of people. The small island nation of the Maldives in the Indian Ocean lies barely above sea level. Rising sea levels due to climate change threaten to inundate the home of more than three hundred thousand people who themselves contribute little to the problem of climate change. This disproportionality between those primarily responsible for global climate change and those who must bear the devastating consequences renders global climate change one of the great justice issues of our time. Recall which groups were most affected when Hurricane Katrina devastated New Orleans in 2005. I don't recall seeing images of wealthy white people sitting on rooftops, desperately awaiting rescue!

The same argument can be made for the issue of biodiversity loss, one of the least talked about but most important of all environmental concerns. We are quickly entering a period of mass extinction caused by habitat destruction, pollution, climate change, and the introduction of invasive species. Species of organisms we will never know (mostly in the rainforest) disappear every day, and we stand to lose 25 to 50 percent of all species by the end of this century if we do not make drastic changes to our way of life. Why do these species not have as much right to life on earth as humans have? Why is it considered acceptable for humans to run polar bears, spotted owls, and all manner of other creatures into extinction? If God is the author of all life on the planet, then other creatures have just as much right to life as do humans. So the mass extinction of all these other magnificent life forms as a result of activities by one species, *homo sapiens*, is clearly an issue of justice.

When considering the relationship between justice and the environment, we cannot ignore the very real presence of environmental racism. Where do toxic waste dumps and other types of hazardous industrial complexes get built? Generally in close proximity to poor neighborhoods largely populated by minority groups. I doubt you will find coal-fired power plants in the direct vicinity of mansions in the Hamptons. Those with resources and the power such resources bestow can assure a safe, clean living environment for themselves inside their gated communities, but only at the expense of poorer communities who lack the political power to resist the environmental degradation of their own neighborhoods. Environmental hazards must be placed somewhere. Environmental racism is therefore a fundamental question of justice.

So if global climate change, biodiversity loss, and environmental racism are all questions of justice, then Christians and Muslims worthy to be called Christians and Muslims must speak up prophetically in the face of the obvious environmental injustices we see all around us. Some do, but why don't more? One reason may be that environmental concerns are not explicitly addressed in either the Bible or the Qur'an. This is not surprising, of course. There were no environmental problems in the ancient world that produced these scriptural texts. Neither Jesus nor Muhammad could foresee a time when human population and consumption levels would grow to such an extent that the natural systems of the planet that sustain life would be strained to the breaking point. Environmental problems result directly from the tripling of the human population during the twentieth century, making this a uniquely modern problem, and one for which neither the Qur'an nor the Bible provides specific guidance. We have to figure this out for ourselves. But doing so should not be difficult. The Bible and the Qur'an both represent prophetic calls for justice, and the fundamental question of justice, as we have seen, is at the heart of all forms of environmental degradation.

Unfortunately, the Christian failure in this regard has been truly monumental, at least in America. Recall the earlier example of Illinois Congressman John Shimkus, whose anti–climate change stance is based on a literal reading of a couple of carefully selected biblical passages that seem to suggest God will never again destroy the world. (Of course, the issue of climate change is not about what God will or will not do but about what humans are doing!) Shimkus's view, shared unfortunately by many other Christians, rises nearly to the level of self-caricature. (*South Park* would be hard pressed to do it any better!) Recall also the work of Stephanie Hendricks, who has documented so well the marriage between antienvironmental political actors and certain forms of evangelical Christianity. Not all Christians are antienvironmental—not by a long shot. But the Christians who are have enjoyed a disproportionate influence on the political process, rendering impossible the enactment of any kind of meaningful legislation to curb greenhouse-gas emissions. If antienvironmental evangelicals actually understood their Bible, they would be prophetically shouting from the rooftops for a carbon tax and for massive investment in clean renewable energy. The silence is deafening.

For their part, Muslims have not been so much antienvironmental as just quiet on the matter. As Tariq Ramadan puts it, the importance afforded the created order as a form of divine revelation in the Qur'an

> should be enough to convince us of the importance of the Creation and of nature in the Islamic universe of reference. However, reality seems to suggest that this is not the case and that reflection about respecting the environment or about how animals should be treated is virtually nonexistent in contemporary Islamic intellectual discourse.[26]

Environmental concerns have clearly not been much on the radar screens of Muslim thinkers, and little effort that I am aware of has been spent seeking qur'anic guidance on issues like global climate change or biodiversity loss. Instead, Ramadan complains,

> Consciences are stifled by heaps of legal rulings, *fatawa* which address formal or secondary issues (such as, for instance, the strictly lawful character of ritual slaughter techniques in the production of meat), without considering far deeper issues such as reflection over ways of life and modes of behavior and consumption.[27]

Essentially, Ramadan charges Muslims with being too caught up in superficial issues of religious-identity obsession to be able to engage deeper issues of environmental destruction and sustainability. Ramadan, of course, is one Muslim—and he may be the first—to take environmental issues seriously and to articulate a response informed by Islamic sources. Fortunately, he is not alone.

The year 2010 witnessed the publication of the book *Green Deen: What Islam Teaches about Protecting the Planet*, by Ibrahim Abdul-Matin, an environmental-policy consultant who has worked with the New York City mayor's office. This book also bears a foreword by Keith Ellison, a Muslim congressman from Minnesota. Muslims may be a bit late to the

26. Ramadan, *Radical Reform*, 233.

27. Ibid., 234.

environmental movement, but at least there is now evidence of a Muslim prophetic voice beginning to stir that recognizes the relationship between environmental destruction and the fundamental questions of justice that Muslims are called to engage.

Unlike Muslim environmental activism, Christian environmental activism has a long legacy stretching back to the very beginnings of the environmental movement in the 1960s. The names are too numerous to mention but would read like a who's who of Christian academic theologians and ethicists. These thinkers have produced a veritable library's worth of literature expounding on the Christian responsibility to care for God's creation and to address the issues of injustice at the heart of environmental problems. But because these prophetic voices have existed largely in the academic world, they have failed in many instances to filter down to the laity so that environmental activism could become a mainstay of local-church activity. Despite the efforts of the last fifty years, how many pastors today preach sermons about global climate change or environmental racism (even on the Sunday closest to Earth Day)? A few undoubtedly do, but all should. Hesitancy in this regard is clearly motivated, at least in part, by an unwillingness among many pastors to appear too political in the pulpit. Proclaiming God's care for the environment gets branded as advocacy of a liberal political agenda. Better to just avoid this potential minefield. But while pastors ignore the minefield, the mines keep exploding all around us in the form of dramatically altered weather patterns and accelerating rates of extinction. Given the political influence of the antienvironmental Christians, Christians in general (especially those liberal ones!) have much work to do to reclaim a prophetic voice on what could arguably be considered the most important issue of our time—the very sustainability of life on earth.

If Muslims and Christians can find a way to come together and wage a responsible jihad against economic, gender, and racial injustice, there is no reason why they cannot do so when it comes to environmental injustice. Environmental problems are closely tied to economic exploitation of natural resources and the overconsumptive lifestyle enjoyed by those in consumer economies. Resisting economic injustice will automatically have a positive effect on natural ecosystems as more and more people turn to spiritual rather than material forms of fulfillment. Likewise, if we take seriously Elisabeth Schüssler Fiorenza's critique of *kyriarchy* as the cause of gender injustice, we will be in a perfect position to advocate for justice for the more-than-human world since hierarchical structures of domination are a root cause of human exploitation of the natural world. Biodiversity loss can probably not be reversed without this fundamental change in attitude away from hierarchy and toward mutual caring. Finally, any attempt to address racism will automatically have to take account of environmental racism as one of racism's most pernicious forms. So waging a responsible jihad against the looming environmental crisis need not be an activity separate from other forms of jihad. Systems of injustice are deeply intertwined and call for comprehensive forms of prophetic resistance.

Therefore, Christians and Muslims have no excuse to sit idly by while global climate patterns become permanently altered, as species are driven to extinction at an alarming rate, and as marginalized communities are made to bear the debilitating consequences of exposure to toxic waste. Islam and Christianity have both historically affirmed the natural environment as a source of revelation about God. As the Qur'an says,

> Do they not look at the sky above them—
>   how we have built it and made it beautiful and free of all faults?
> And the earth—We have spread it wide, and set upon it mountains firm,
>   and caused it to bring forth plants of all beauteous kinds,
> thus offering an insight and a reminder unto every human being who
>   willingly turns unto God. (50:6–8)

Muslims and Christians must raise their prophetic voices before it is too late to save the planet from becoming unfit for life. Nothing could be more consistent with Christian and Muslim identity than engaging in a full-bodied environmental activism. This does not mean simply hugging a tree; it will require full-scale political engagement informed by a spiritual understanding of every organism as a unique creation of God with full rights to life and prosperity. Again the Qur'an reminds us:

> There is no creature that walks on earth,
>   no bird that flies on its two wings
> but has a community of its own like yours.
> Nothing has been left out of Our recording;
>   unto their Lord they shall all be gathered. (6:38)

The Qur'an affirms the moral equivalence of human and more-than-human creatures. Environmental concerns are a matter of justice. This is one jihad we can ill afford to ignore.

JESUS AND JIHAD

WAGING A JIHAD FOR A JUST PEACE

Everyone claims to want a more peaceful world. The twentieth century, with its two world wars and multiple genocides, is often considered the most violent century in history. The twenty-first is not getting off to such a great start either, with its multiple civil wars and terrorism. We long for a time of peace. But if everyone truly yearns for a more peaceful world, why do we continue to perpetuate so much violence? The answer may lie in the often overlooked connection between peace and justice. We tend to define peace as the absence of conflict and therefore make the striving for peace our primary goal: If we can just find a way to end wars and stop the terrorists from killing us, the world will be at peace. But history shows that striving for peace by trying to end conflict usually leads to more conflict. The circle does not end. And this is because conflict is not a primary problem, it is the mere side effect of deeply entrenched systems of injustice. People don't normally engage in violent conflict just for the sake of conflict. They engage in violent conflict because they feel they have been the victim of a deep injustice.

Take the 9/11 attacks, for example. Al-Qaeda did not develop a strong anti-American ideology and then act on that ideology by pulling off a horrendous display of violence just for the sake of killing Americans. They were responding, rightly or wrongly, to what they saw as a deep and abiding injustice perpetuated by America on Muslim lands in the form of America's heavy-handed military presence in the Middle East and its unfettered support for the Israeli occupation of Palestinian territories. America's response to the 9/11 attacks—the invasion of two sovereign nations leading to the deaths of tens of thousands of people and the continuing drone strikes that kill the innocent—was likewise not motivated by a desire for conflict but by the attempt to respond to a perceived injustice: the wanton slaughter of almost three thousand innocent Americans. The way to bring about peace is not to focus on ending conflict. The way to bring about peace is to work for justice. Peace follows justice, not the other way around.

Muslim scholar Farid Esack makes this point well. Commenting on the aftermath of 9/11 he states,

> While progressive Muslims shared the revulsion of others at
> the death of innocents, they display a much more cynical at-
> titude towards an uncritiqued peace discourse. For progressive
> Muslims, "real peace" seems to be one that follows the creation
> of a just world. In contrast, a seemingly ideology-less peace that,

uncritiqued, translates into acquiescence to a new corporate dominated world—most starkly represented by the United States of
America—is one to be not only avoided but also opposed. Dominant empires develop an ideological rooted interest in peace which
reinforces a *status quo* that may very well be an unjust one, as Paul
Salem points out: "Conflict and bellicosity is useful—indeed essential—in building empires, but an ideology of peace and conflict
resolution is clearly more appropriate for its maintenance." When
we fail to raise critical questions about the *status quo* that requires
peace then we run the risk of becoming a part of the problem.[28]

Recall how the Roman Empire resorted to brutal displays of military power
to enforce the *Pax Romana*, the Peace of Rome. The empire had a rooted
interest in stamping out conflict in order to maintain the stability of its unjust economic system. Absence of conflict was a prerequisite to continuing
injustice. Can the same be said for America's attempts to maintain peace
and stability in the world? Does the *Pax Americana* serve unjust ends?

However you answer that last question, it is clear that there can be no
lasting peace in the world without the development of just political, economic, and social systems. To be a force for peace, Christians and Muslims
must consider waging a responsible jihad against all forms of injustice. But
this is made difficult by the pernicious continuation of Religious-Identity
Obsession Syndrome in both communities. Virtually all Muslims worldwide when asked to name an example of a systemic injustice of particular
importance to them will raise up the plight of the Palestinian people. And
they are correct to do this. Palestinians *are* victims of an unjust Western-
supported Israeli occupation that oppresses them terribly. But how many
Muslims will also mention the plight of the North Korean people, oppressed by a brutal dictatorial regime. Or the plight of Coptic Christians in
Egypt, who often suffer at the hands of the Muslim majority? Or the *Wall
Street Journal* reporter Daniel Pearl, who was brutally murdered by Islamic
extremists in Pakistan? Too many Muslims focus only on the victimhood of
fellow Muslims rather than resisting all forms of injustice, no matter the religious identity of the victims. Recall how the Emir Abd-el-Kader defended
his fellow Muslims when they were victimized by French Christians but
intervened to save the lives of Christians when they were being killed by
his fellow Muslims. This is the spirit that must animate any jihad for a just
peace.

28. Esack, "In Search of Progressive Islam beyond 9/11," 84.

Christians, of course, struggle too with Religious-Identity Obsession Syndrome. The development of Christian Zionism is a perfect example of the syndrome. Some evangelical Christians, based on their belief that Israel's flowering in the Middle East represents the fulfillment of biblical prophecy, hold to the divine right of Israel to rule the land of Palestine, and if they can see this prophecy being fulfilled before their very eyes, they can believe in other aspects of so-called biblical prophecy as well. Christian Zionism is nothing more than a self-serving delusion of so-called Christians so caught up in superficial religious-identity obsessions that they have become blind to the blatant injustices suffered by the Palestinian people at the hands of the Israeli occupation and deaf to the true prophetic witness of Jesus to struggle against all forms of injustice, no matter the religious identity of the victims. Despite its incongruence with the gospel message, Religious-Identity Obsession Syndrome persists among Christians.

Several years ago, I received a Christmas letter written by the very pious wife of a former seminary colleague. She related a trip she had taken through several Middle Eastern countries with a group of other pastors and asked the recipients of her letter to please pray for the *Christians* in the Middle East. But why only for the Christians! Don't Muslims, Jews, and others need our prayers too? Apparently not in the opinion of those blinded to the prophetic call to care for all people of the earth by Religious-Identity Obsession Syndrome.

At its best, a responsible jihad will constitute a global movement of non-violent resistance against all forms of injustice—a movement led by Muslims, Christians, and others who have developed spiritual roots deep enough to allow them to see beyond narrowly drawn religious-identity labels and strong enough to allow them to advocate for justice and for the dignity of every person on the globe. Striving for justice will in the end result in the peaceful world we all so much crave. It is high time to wage a jihad for a just peace.

I began this book by highlighting the courage of a young Muslim man unafraid to stand up for justice and exercise a prophetic voice, a Muslim man with the temerity to stand in a federal courtroom and equate the American Revolution with jihad. I end with a plea for all Muslims and Christians to follow the lead of Tarek Mehanna, for jihad is not only a concept uniquely suited to describe the founding of the American republic, but also a concept uniquely suited to characterize the mission of Jesus of Nazareth. All Christians and Muslims are called to wage a responsible jihad in resistance to the multitude of injustices we see around us every day. But, of course, Tarek Mehanna is in jail. How can he wage a jihad from behind prison bars?

This is a crucial question. The deeply Islamophobic character of American society—and increasingly of much of the world—places any Muslim who dares whisper the dreaded *j* word under immediate suspicion and liable to preemptive prosecution and imprisonment. Any talk of jihad, any attempt to advocate for justice, any desire to upset the status quo, places Muslims in an extremely vulnerable and increasingly dangerous position. For this reason, Muslims cannot be expected to lead a global jihad against injustice. The onus, instead, falls on Christians to take up the mantle of leadership.

Recently I spoke at a conference where I made the argument that America was greatly in need of the twin Islamic concepts of *tawhid* and jihad. The Muslim scholar who followed my presentation confessed his amazement with the words, "I could never get away with saying that America needed *tawhid* and jihad," to which I replied, "I know you can't say it; that's why I have to." Christians will need to claim ownership of the Jesus/jihad connection while reclaiming their own fading prophetic voice in order for any jihad to get off the ground. Once a jihad for justice is underway, however, Muslims can join in, working with all who have a passion for justice to reshape the world in a way that promotes the dignity of every human and every more-than-human life form inhabiting the planet. The task will not be easy, but the consequences of not trying could prove disastrous. This is not a choice we have to make, for we really have no choice; this is a responsibility we cannot avoid even if we try. Our task is simply to respond to the prophetic call for justice staring at us from every corner of the Islamic and Christian traditions. In this spirit, I leave you with the words spoken to me by a Muslim colleague upon hearing about the harsh Islamophobic reaction I received in response to my earlier work—the words were, "Welcome to the jihad!"

Bibliography

Abdul-Matin, Ibrahim. *Green Deen: What Islam Teaches about Protecting the Planet*. San Francisco: Berrett-Koehler, 2010.

Afzaal, Ahmed. *Jihad without Violence*. Warren, MI: Islamic Organization of North America, 2010.

Ahmad, Israr. *Islamic Renaissance: The Real Task Ahead*. 6th ed. Lahore: Markazi Anjuman Khuddan-ul-Qur'an, 2001.

———. *Obligations to God: A Comprehensive Islamic View*. Lahore: Markazi Anjuman Khuddan-ul-Qur'an, 2002.

———. *Rise and Decline of the Muslim Ummah*. Lahore: Markazi Anjuman Khuddan-ul-Qur'an, 1991.

Algar, Hamid, trans. *Islam and Revolution: Writings and Declarations of Imam Khomeini*. Contemporary Islamic Thought. Persian Series. Berkeley: Mizan, 1981.

Asad, Muhammad. *The Message of the Qur'an*. Bristol, UK: Book Foundation, 2003.

Barash, David. "The Hardest Problem in Science?" *The Chronicle of Higher Education*, October 28, 2011. http://chronicle.com/blogs/brainstorm/the-hardest-problem-in-science/40845/.

Batnitzky, Leora. *How Judaism Became a Religion: An Introduction to Modern Jewish Thought*. Princeton: Princeton University Press, 2011.

Bonney, Richard. *Jihad: From Qur'an to Bin Laden*. New York: Palgrave, 2004.

Bostom, Andrew, ed. *The Legacy of Jihad: Islamic Holy War and the Fate of Non-Muslims*. Amherst, NY: Prometheus, 2005.

Bouyerdene, Ahmed. *Emir Abd el-Kader: Hero and Saint of Islam*. Translated and introduced by Gustavo Polit. Bloomington, IN: World Wisdom, 2012.

Caputi, Ross. "If Tarek Mehanna Is Guilty So Am I." *Common Dreams*, April 16, 2012, http://www.commondreams.org/views/2012/04/16/if-tarek-mehanna-guilty-so-am-i/.

Chapra, M. Umar. "The Islamic Welfare State." In *Islam in Transition: Muslim Perspectives*, edited by John J. Donahue and John L. Esposito, 242–48. 2nd ed. New York: Oxford University Press, 2007.

Cone, James H. *God of the Oppressed*. San Francisco: HarperSanFrancisco, 1975.

Crossan, John Dominic. *The Historical Jesus: The Life of a Mediterranean Jewish Peasant*. San Francisco: HarperSanFrancisco, 1992.

———. "Roman Imperial Theology." In *In the Shadow of Empire: Reclaiming the Bible as a History of Faithful Resistance*, edited by Richard A. Horsley, 59–74. Louisville: Westminster John Knox, 2008.

Bibliography

Donner, Fred M. *Muhammad and the Believers: At the Origins of Islam*. Cambridge, MA: Belknap, 2010.

Eliade, Mircea. *The Sacred and the Profane: The Nature of Religion*. Translated by Willard R. Trask. New York: Harcourt, Brace, 1959.

Elliott, John H. "Jesus the Israelite Was Neither a 'Jew' nor a 'Christian': On Correcting Misleading Nomenclature." *Journal for the Study of the Historical Jesus* 5.2 (2007) 119–54.

Esack, Farid. "In Search of Progressive Islam beyond 9/11." In *Progressive Muslims: On Justice, Gender, and Pluralism*, edited by Omid Safi, 78–97. Oxford: Oneworld, 2003.

———. *On Being a Muslim: Finding a Religious Path in the World Today*. Oxford: Oneworld, 1999.

Firestone, Reuven. *Jihad: The Origin of Holy War in Islam*. New York: Oxford University Press, 1999.

Fitzgerald, Timothy. *The Ideology of Religious Studies*. New York: Oxford University Press, 2000.

Francis I, Pope. *Evangelii Gaudium*. http://www.vatican.va/evangelii-gaudium/en/.

Frattaroli, Elio. *Healing the Soul in the Age of the Brain: Why Medication Isn't Enough*. New York: Penguin, 2002.

French, Rose. "Grace Church Pastor, Flock Find New Home with Like-minded White Congregation in South St. Paul." *Twin Cities Star-Tribune*, September 29, 2013. http://www.startribune.com/local/south/225666931.html/.

Galbraith, James K. *Inequality and Instability: A Study of the World Economy Just before the Great Crisis*. New York: Oxford University Press, 2012.

Greenberg, Gary. *The Book of Woe: The DSM and the Unmasking of Psychiatry*. New York: Blue Rider, 2013.

Greenwald, Glenn. "The Real Criminals in the Tarek Mehanna Case." *Salon*, Friday, April 13, 2012. http://www.salon.com/2012/04/13/the_real_criminals_in_the_tarek_mehanna_case/.

Guillaume, Alfred. *The Life of Muhammad: A Translation of Ibn Ishaq's Sirat Rasul Allah*. London: Oxford University Press, 1955.

Gutiérrez, Gustavo. *A Theology of Liberation: History, Politics, and Salvation*. Translated and edited by Sister Caridad Inda and John Eagleson. Maryknoll, NY: Orbis, 1973.

Hamer, Dean H, *The God Gene: How Faith Is Hardwired into Our Genes*. New York: Doubleday, 2004.

Hanson, K. C. "How Honorable! How Shameful! A Cultural Analysis of Matthew's Makarisms and Reproaches." *Semeia* 67 (1996) 81–111.

Hendricks, Stephanie. *Divine Destruction: Wise Use, Dominion Theology, and the Making of American Environmental Policy*. Melville Manifestos. Hoboken, NJ: Melville House, 2005.

Horsley, Richard A., ed. *In the Shadow of Empire: Reclaiming the Bible as a History of Faithful Resistance*. Louisville: Westminster John Knox, 2008.

———. *Jesus and Empire: The Kingdom of God and the New World Disorder*. Minneapolis: Fortress, 2003.

———. *Jesus and the Spiral of Violence: Popular Jewish Resistance in Roman Palestine*. 1987. Reprinted, Minneapolis: Fortress, 1993.

Horsley, Richard A., and John S. Hanson. *Bandits, Prophets, and Messiahs: Popular Movements in the Time of Jesus*. 1985. Reprinted, Harrisburg, PA: Trinity, 1999.

Bibliography

Islahi, Amin Ahsan. "Self-Development in the Context of Man's Relationship with Allah." In *Tazkiyah: The Islamic Path of Self-Development*, edited by Abdur Rashid Siddiqui, 133–214. Leicestershire, UK: Islamic Foundation, 2004.

Josephson, Jason Ananda. *The Invention of Religion in Japan*. Chicago: University of Chicago Press, 2012.

Jung, C. G. *Memories, Dreams, Reflections*. Recorded and edited by Aniela Jaffé. Translated by Richard and Clara Winston. New York: Vintage, 1965.

Kepel, Gilles. *The Trail of Political Islam*. Translated by Anthony F. Roberts. Cambridge, MA: Belknap, 2002.

Khan, Ruqayya Y. "Did a Woman Edit the Qur'an? Hafsa and Her Famed 'Codex.'" *Journal of the American Academy of Religion* 82 (2014) 174–215.

Kiser, John W. *Commander of the Faithful: The Life and Times of Emir Abd el-Kader; A Life of True Jihad*. Rhinebeck, NY: Monkfish, 2008.

Krugman, Paul. "Plutocrats Feeling Persecuted." *New York Times*, September 26, 2013. http://www.nytimes.com/2013/09/27/opinion/krugman-plutocrats-feeling-persecuted.html?_r=0/.

Lean, Nathan. *The Islamophobia Industry: How the Right Manufactures Fear of Muslims*. London: Pluto, 2012.

Lings, Martin. *Muhammad: His Life Based on the Earliest Sources*. Rochester, VT: Inner Traditions, 1983.

Mahmud, Mustafa. "Islam vs. Marxism and Capitalism." In *Islam in Transition: Muslim Perspectives*, edited by John J. Donahue and John L. Esposito, 128–32. 2nd ed. New York: Oxford University Press, 2007.

Malina, Bruce J. "'Religion' in the World of Paul." *Biblical Theology Bulletin* 16 (1986) 92–101.

Mandela, Nelson. *Long Walk to Freedom*. Boston: Little, Brown, 1994.

Marston, Elsa. *The Compassionate Warrior: Abd el-Kader of Algeria*. Bloomington, IN: Wisdom Tales, 2013.

Mason, Steve. "Jews, Judaeans, Judaizing, Judaism: Problems of Categorization in Ancient History." *Journal for the Study of Judaism* 38 (2007) 457–512.

Masuzawa, Tomoko. *The Invention of World Religions*. Chicago: University of Chicago Press, 2005.

National Council of Churches of Christ in the United States of America, Division of Christian Education. *The Holy Bible: New Revised Standard Version*. Nashville: Nelson, 1989.

Newberg, Andrew et al. *Why God Won't Go Away: Brain Science and the Biology of Belief*. New York: Ballantine, 2001.

Oakman, Douglas E. *Jesus and the Peasants*. Matrix. Eugene, OR: Cascade Books, 2008.

———. *Jesus, Debt, and the Lord's Prayer*. Eugene, OR: Cascade Books, 2014.

Qutb, Sayyid. *Milestones*. Translated by Ahmad Zaki Hammad. Indianapolis: American Trust Publications, 1990.

Rackham, H., trans. *Pliny: Natural History*, vol. 5. Loeb Classical Library. Cambridge: Harvard University Press, 1946.

Rahman, Fazlur. *Major Themes of the Qur'an*. Minneapolis: Biblioteca Islamica, 1980.

Ramadan, Tariq. *Radical Reform: Islamic Ethics and Liberation*. New York: Oxford University Press, 2009.

———. *Western Muslims and the Future of Islam*. New York: Oxford University Press, 2004.

Bibliography

Rauschenbusch, Walter. *Christianity and the Social Crisis in the 21st Century*, with essays by Tony Campolo et al. Edited by Paul Rauschenbusch. New York: HarperOne, 2007.

Rippen, Andrew. "Witness to Faith." In *Encyclopaedia of the Qur'an*, edited by Jane Dammen McAulife, 5:488–91. 6 vols. Leiden: Brill, 2006.

Satel, Sally, and Scott O. Lilienfield. *Brainwashed: The Seductive Appeal of Mindless Neuroscience*. New York: Basic Books, 2013.

Shah-Khazemi, Reza. "From the Spirituality of Jihad to the Ideology of Jihadism." In *Islam, Fundamentalism, and the Betrayal of Tradition*, edited by Joseph E. P. Lumbard, 119–48. Rev. ed. The Perennial Philosophy Series. Bloomington, IN: World Wisdom, 2009.

Shaikh, Sa'diyya. "Transforming Feminisms: Islam, Women, and Gender Justice." In *Progressive Muslims: On Justice, Gender, and Pluralism*, edited by Omid Safi, 147–62. Oxford: Oneworld, 2003.

Shedinger, Robert F. *Radically Open: Transcending Religious Identity in an Age of Anxiety*. Eugene, OR: Cascade Books, 2012.

———. *Was Jesus a Muslim? Questioning Categories in the Study of Religion*. Minneapolis: Fortress, 2009.

Southern Poverty Law Center. "Hate Group Numbers Up by 54% since 2000." February 26, 2009. http://www.splcenter.org/get-informed/news/hate-group-numbers-up

Stiglitz, Joseph E. *The Price of Inequality: How Today's Divided Society Endangers Our Future*. New York: Norton, 2012.

Taha, Mahmoud Mohamed. *The Second Message of Islam*. Translated by Abdullahi Ahmed An-Na'im. Contemporary Issues in the Middle East. Syracuse: Syracuse University Press, 1987.

Taylor, Charles. *A Secular Age*. Cambridge, MA: Belknap, 2007.

Thackeray, H. St. J., trans. *Josephus*. Vol. 3, *The Jewish War*. Loeb Classical Library. Cambridge: Harvard University Press, 1928.

Tibi, Bassam. *Islamism and Islam*. New Haven: Yale University Press, 2012.

Wadud, Amina. *Inside the Gender Jihad: Women's Reform in Islam*. Oxford: Oneworld, 2006.

Whitaker, Robert. *Anatomy of an Epidemic: Magic Bullets, Psychiatric Drugs, and the Astonishing Rise of Mental Illness in America*. New York: Crown, 2010.

Wright, Robert B. "Psalms of Solomon." In *The Old Testament Pseudepigrapha*, edited by James H. Charlesworth, 2:639–72. 2 vols. Garden City, NY: Doubleday, 1985.